Bale Out

Escaping Occupied France with the Resistance

Alfie Martin

Regards Tom

Alfie Martin

Febr 2010

Colourpoint Books

6 5 4 3 2 1

© Alfie Martin and Colourpoint Books
  Newtownards 2009
Originally published 2005
This edition published 2009

Designed by Colourpoint Books,
Newtownards
Printed on demand by Lulu.com

ISBN 978-1-906578-51-0

Colourpoint Books
Jubilee Business Park
Jubilee Road
NEWTOWNARDS
County Down
Northern Ireland
BT23 4YH
Tel: 028 9182 6339
Fax: 028 9182 1900
E-mail: info@colourpoint.co.uk
Web-site: www.colourpoint.co.uk

Alfie Martin is a Belfast man. He was born at Finaghy in 1920 and was educated at Friends School, Lisburn, before taking up employment with the Liverpool & London & Globe Insurance Company (now an almost forgotten part of the Royal Sun Alliance Group), at Wellington Place, Belfast on 20 July 1936.

In January 1939 he joined a Territorial Army company of Royal Engineers. Called up in August that year he served at Kilroot, Helen's Bay and Magilligan before joining the Royal Air Force in May 1941.

Cover Picture: Halifax HR 663 of No 102 Squadron RAF in flames over Epsauvage, Belgium on the night of 16/17 April 1943, from a painting by *Norman Whitla.*

Contents

This book is dedicated to the Resistance workers, of many countries, who risked their lives to help airmen, and others, escape, or evade capture, during World War 2.

Members of the Royal Air Forces Escaping Society refer to these individuals as 'helpers'. Typically they are ordinary (or extraordinary) people, such as those who visited Canada in 1967, its Centennial Year, as guests of the Canadian Branch of the RAFES. At that time I had the honour to be Chairman of the Branch. Brief details about each of these 'helpers' can be found on pages 94 and 95.

Chapter 1:
The beginning, and all is well

My family had lived in the Finaghy area, on the southern outskirts of Belfast, for many generations. They were farmers, cattle dealers, milk producers and cess collectors. My mother, however, was from Pudsey, a small village near Leeds, Yorkshire, where her family had interests in the woollen trade. It was on holiday in the Isle of Man that my father and mother met, so when they married in 1913 she became somewhat isolated from her six brothers and two sisters.

I arrived in 1920, born at home, probably with the help of a doctor and/or midwife, although, not unusually, I remember nothing. However, I do know that we had a live-in nurse for a short period, because she became a friend of the family and visited us from time to time thereafter. When, and if, we complain about the National Health Service we would do well to remember the somewhat primitive practices of the past. Indeed one of my early memories is of having my tonsils removed whilst lying on our kitchen table; I was about five at the time. A normal recovery was made, marred only by an eruption of blood all over the bed, shortly after the operation.

Looking back, I remember a happy and contented childhood. My parents were, in my opinion, well adjusted and acted in a completely responsible way towards me, my elder sister, Dorothy, and my younger brother, Bobby. The latter, unfortunately, was what is now known as a Downs Syndrome child but at the time he was described as suffering from convulsions. Our parents gave us all a great deal of affection, which we returned. Bobby, in particular, got much loving care and turned out to be a very happy person. Whilst he never worked, he was well trained by my parents and later attended special schools. Known to almost everyone in the neighbourhood, his main interests were music, the church and the buses. Perhaps, I can take this belated opportunity to thank the drivers and conductors of Belfast Corporation buses for their friendliness towards Bobby when he travelled in and out of the city as a kind of unpaid additional employee.

Schooling began when I was three and a half years of age. My sister took my hand on the first day, and we walked the half mile to Malone Public Elementary School on Balmoral Avenue. I cannot remember much about the teachers, but 'Bouf' Rea was the Headmaster, 'Ma' Agnew was my first teacher and a Miss Cupples was in charge of the second class. Mr Rea was a good teacher and the school was well run. Perhaps he had some leanings towards religion, as I seem to remember that he believed that there would be a 'second coming' about the mid 1930s. When I was aged about seven, and in Miss Cupples class, I remember being hit over the knuckles with a cane, because of some misdemeanour on my part. I cried a little whereupon I was hugged and given a kiss by Miss Cupples. Such indignity was enough to make any young boy give up crying forever!

Further memories of those early days at school include a large addition being made to the original small building, which faced onto Balmoral Avenue. Evidently there was a growing school population coming from substantial housing developments in the area. About the same time the dirt and gravel road beyond the tram lines, and leading to Finaghy and Dunmurry, was relaid in concrete. It vastly improved our opportunities to slide most of the way to school on those frosty winter mornings. Traffic on the roads was light and varied – cars and small lorries, delivery bicycles, bread and milk carts, one battery driven car, horses and hearses, ponies and traps and cattle being driven to market and the relatively new double-deck electric trams travelling back and forth across the city.

School days at Malone were very pleasant and I believe that I made good progress. At the Christmas, Easter and June tests and examinations I did quite well and managed to stay near to the top of the class. My chief rival, and lifelong friend, was Charlie Hicks (also later Royal Air Force and recently with Sirocco and Northern Ireland Electricity).

Rain or shine, we walked, or ran, to school, back home for dinner (lunch) and home once more about 3.30pm, hoping that the homework would not take long. On the warm days at the end of May it was always a lovely diversion when homeward bound to explore the Royal Ulster Agricultural Society Show. I cannot remember whether or not we got in free, but if not it must have been very reasonable as our weekly allowance ranged from nothing to three old pence. Once inside we visited and saw everything. In particular we were attracted to the free samples, which were, most often, leaflets advertising farm machinery, feeding stuffs or fertilisers – the three Fs of an innocent and orderly world.

In 1931 it was time to move towards higher things and, after obtaining a scholarship worth about £15.00 per annum, I followed my sister to Friends' School, Lisburn. My father had attended Inst (the Royal Belfast Academical Institution) and I think he would have liked to send me there, but finances did not permit. Whilst he never spoke about it, and never complained, he had suffered great loss in the troubles of 1921. Shortly before that time he and a partner had set up a new printing business on the Springfield Road. It was burnt out. Then, as now, fire insurance did not cover riot damage and there was no government compensation. However, as a traveller for printing and stationery he managed to keep our family in comfort, if not in luxury, and I feel we thrived on it.

Friends' School, on Prospect Hill in Lisburn, had about 130 pupils at that time, of which about half were Quakers and many were boarders. The day pupils, of which I was one, mixed very happily with the others, but possibly we were a little in the 'second division' as we did not partake in all the school activities, homework sessions, meals, church outings, etc. Sports were compulsory and enjoyed by most according to their abilities. The boys played rugby in the autumn term, hockey in the winter term and cricket after Easter. Our teams were not very good, except at hockey where the competition was not so great. However, there was the compensation that due to lack of numbers if you were old enough, or big enough, you had no trouble making the First XV or First XI. For a school of our size we had excellent facilities – ample playing fields adjacent to the school and good changing facilities (but lacking hot showers). The school even had an indoor swimming bath which, next to the North Pole, was about the coldest place on earth.

These were not the days when Mummy dropped off and picked up little Johnny in the second family car. Three or four of us from the Finaghy area travelled to and from school in Lisburn by train, a distance of about four miles. Indeed the frequency and efficiency of the service was such that we were able to travel home for lunch and return within the allotted time of 75 minutes. Obviously the cost of a season ticket for the train was more economical than buying meals at a café or at school. Taking sandwiches and a Thermos was not as yet common.

I started at Friends' in the Upper Fourth, with about 16 others. We progressed through Lower Fifth to Upper Fifth where we sat for the Junior Certificate Examinations (roughly the equivalent of 'O' levels). At this stage about half the pupils left and it was a small form of eight that went on to Lower Sixth, and finally Upper Sixth. We had our final examination for Senior Certificate ('A' level) which most of us passed. In my case I got through by the faintest of margins but, since I was only 16, it was enough. In a less demanding world I might have sat again the following year hoping for better marks, but the country was still in depression and that dictated that I should find a job and earn some money.

This was June 1936 and family circumstances meant that I should look for a job. Attending university would be too expensive for my parents, and, in any case, at that time only about 3% of final school leavers went to university. Early in July I replied to an advertisement for a job as a Junior Clerk with an insurance company. A few days later I was interviewed (successfully) and commenced work with the Liverpool & London & Globe Insurance Company Ltd at 25 Wellington Place, Belfast on 20 July 1936.

A requirement of the position had been secondary education standard of Senior Certificate. The results of the examination which

I had taken in June were issued in August and I was very relieved to learn that I had passed, although only by the skin of my teeth. The subject that I nearly failed was French. Three years passed, I liked my job and progressed from Junior Clerk (licker of stamps, etc) to Accident Department Clerk (policy and endorsement drafting and underwriting), to Junior Inspector with the task of developing business in the counties of Fermanagh, Cavan and Monaghan.

In the late 1930s life was pleasant for an employed teenager earning something in the region of £50–60 per year. There were dances and local 'hops' to attend each Saturday evening and, in my case, golf in the evenings during the week. Balmoral Golf Club was one of the clubs which was beginning to encourage juveniles. As one of those I found my way onto the club's Ulster Cup team and I also had some success in the local competitions. Thanks to a very favourable handicap I managed to win the Match Play Captain's prize in 1937. My daughter and family are now making use of the very handsome tea trolley and cutlery which I won at that time.

Almost unobserved by me things were happening in the world outside. George V had died, Edward VIII had had an affair and abdicated, Hitler and Mussolini had come to power and in Spain there was a civil war. All of these events were ignored by me until the Munich Crisis in 1938. Suddenly I was hit by a great feeling of patriotism and a desire to take some, small, part in the country's move to rearmament. Why I should have felt like this is a mystery. Friends' School had not influenced me, nor my family history or the attitude of my friends. Probably it was just the propaganda and 'spin' of the government at the time.

In November 1938 I went into the RAF recruiting office in Ann Street, Belfast and signed up to join the Volunteer Reserve and "learn to fly at the weekends". It was to be a very short engagement. When I went home and told my parents, my mother in particular was very adamant that I was not to join – it was too dangerous! This was a time when we had great respect for our parents and for their decisions and so that is what I did. The following day I returned to Ann Street and cancelled my application. On reflection I feel sure that my mother's decision saved me from an early fate.

Still feeling that I had to do something towards the government's policy of "Be Prepared", in January 1939 I joined the Antrim Fortress Company, Royal Engineers. This was a Territorial Army company meeting for training one evening a week in a hall in Great Victoria Street, almost opposite to the Grand Opera House. I had the lowly rank of Sapper and received an annual bounty of £5.00. Our Commanding Officer was Major J Maynard Sinclair, later to become Minister of Finance in the Northern Ireland government and later still to lose his life in the *Princess Victoria* ferry disaster in 1953.

The training was mainly based on 1914–1918 requirements – marching, arms drill on the Lee Enfield 303 rifle and Vickers machine gun, trench digging, barbed wire erection, engine and generator operation as required for searchlights. Highlights were a short camping experience in tents and rifle target shooting at Palace Barracks (Holywood) and Ballykinlar. It brought excitement and fun to the young and the not so young, who felt they were helping the country maintain peace or prepare for war.

All during the early months of 1939 efforts continued to satisfy and curtail the territorial ambitions of the fascists led by Hitler, Mussolini, Franco, Mosley and others, but all to no avail as in August the German army occupied Poland. Britain and France laid down an ultimatum which was rejected and Prime Minister Chamberlain declared war on 3 September.

I had been on business in counties Cavan and Monaghan during that last week of August. Returning to Graham's Hotel, Bailieboro on 24 August I received a telegram from my employer (reproduced overleaf) telling me to return immediately and report to the Territorials. Three days were to be spent on personal, family and business affairs before I took a bus to Kilroot and walked the   mile from the main Carrickfergus–Whitehead Road to the camp. That was 28 August 1939. War was declared on 3 September as our troop was on a church parade for the first time. The wireless carried the announcement by the Prime Minister, Neville Chamberlain. We were

Bale Out!

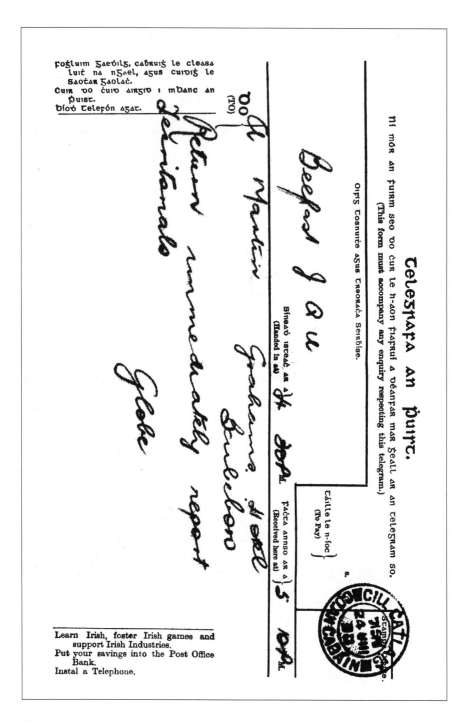

all quite convinced that the war would only last a few weeks but, for those fortunate enough to survive, it was to be at least six years.

All of my time in the army was spent in Northern Ireland, where with my companions, I did my bit on the 'battlefields' of Kilroot, Helen's Bay and Magilligan. Our responsibility was to erect, maintain and service the coastal searchlights and engines required to protect Belfast Lough and the Foyle estuary. It was mainly night duty but we were able to visit our homes frequently and to inspect all the dance halls within a few miles radius. I had purchased a 1928 Standard 9 car for the sum of £7 10s 0d, taxed and insured. The petrol ration was five gallons per month which I was able to supplement with some of the 'juice' used to run our engines. Whilst this was not quite approved of, I think it was overlooked because a number of trips were semi-official, such as bringing officers' families to our church parades. Indeed, at Magilligan, for some time my car was the only form of transport available and it was a long walk from the main road to the Point where we had our searchlights.

Driving in wartime was fun, but the conditions were rather different from today. First there was the blackout which meant you could only use one headlight with a slotted cover. Whilst driving at night your eyes had to become accustomed to the dark and to any helpful moonlight, but there were also the advantages of no oncoming lights and very little traffic. Starting on cold mornings could be a problem as batteries were weak and starting handles uncertain. Whenever possible I parked overnight on a hill, then it was give the car a push, jump in behind the steering wheel, ram it into second gear, let out the clutch and away you'd go. Fuel saving was also very necessary as every drop of petrol was precious. My method was to freewheel at every opportunity. For instance, travelling from Helen's Bay to Belfast I was able to cut off power at the Culloden Hotel and freewheel right into Holywood, almost two miles, a saving of perhaps a quarter of a cup – well who knows.

Life at Magilligan in the summer was like a cross between a boy scout camp and a holiday by the sea. We did a lot of our own cooking over an open fire and I learnt how to find, distinguish and

September 1939 and Sapper Martin, Antrim Fortress Company, Royal Engineers stands amidst the barbed wire at Kilroot, Co Antrim.

cook cockles and mussels, an art which has given me considerable pleasure ever since. My recollections of the time do not include any reference to war, enemy actions or difficult living conditions. All was well, we were young and there must be a dance hall nearby with lots of pretty girls. This was about the time of 'Dunkirk', making it obvious that any sense of wellbeing depended on where you were at the time.

Later in 1940 I was posted back to Helen's Bay to continue the night duties of attending to the generators and the searchlights. Early in 1941 things began to move. Almost all of my companions were posted to Portaferry or Ripon for further training and were never to return. I stayed on wondering what was going to happen to me as I didn't really have much 'engineering' experience. That was my quandary, as I very quietly passed my 21st birthday in March. A few days later I saw a new notice on our information board – the RAF were asking for volunteers for aircrew. That wakened me up. I requested permission to apply from our officers, and duly sent in my application listing Pilot, Observer and Wireless Operator as my preferences in that order.

Almost half of the soldiers in the camp at Helen's Bay had applied, but only four of us were selected for interview. This took place at the RAF Recruiting Office in Clifton Street, Belfast and included a medical examination. I must have satisfied the examiners as at the end of the interview it was suggested to me that I was more suited to train as Observer (Navigation, Bombing and Gunnery). Being most anxious to get away from the Army as I knew it, I accepted the suggestion most eagerly and returned to camp to await my call up. Later I was to wish I had opted for Pilot!

It was not a long wait, just a few weeks, enlivened one night by the blitz on Belfast, which I witnessed from the parade ground at Grey Point, Helen's Bay. Naturally I was concerned for the welfare of my parents, but I could see that most of the raid was concentrated on the docks and the north and east of the city. They lived in the south and were fortunate not to experience the awful death and destruction elsewhere.

Bale Out!

Call up came in May 1941 with the first posting being to the Reception Centre in Stratford-upon-Avon. We were one of the first 'Army Intakes' – 49 of us, billeted in the Shakespeare Hotel, all eager and excited in our new uniforms, white flashes on our forage caps and, wonder of wonders, sheets on our beds. Even the initial training was easy, as all of us had already learnt the drill, the parading and the spit and polish in what was rapidly becoming our 'previous lives'. (Now, I wonder what happened to those old uniforms?)

After a pleasant four weeks our next move was to an Initial Training Wing (ITW) at Scarborough, East Yorkshire where our billet was the Grand Hotel. Here, in addition to drill and physical training, we began to learn a little about aeroplanes, dead reckoning navigation, meteorology, map reading, bombing, gunnery, and signalling. Some examinations followed before we were passed as suitable for further training. Then we were granted seven days leave, which for me meant off to Belfast to stay with my parents and visit the local dance halls. It was also the occasion to see those old friends and colleagues who were still around, to chew the fat with them and probably show off my new uniform and

No 9 Receiving Wing RAF, Flight 3A/18 at Stratford-on-Avon 3 May 1941. I'm in the middle row, on the left.

white aircrew cadet flash – surely, not a step towards the 'glamour boy' image?

During the leave my thoughts were directed to the next step – flying training, but where would it be? South Africa, Rhodesia, Canada, United States or somewhere else in Britain were all possibilities. The answer came with a posting to Wilmslow, Cheshire, which was a transit camp. Our flight was heading to Canada.

Some few days later we boarded the *Ulster Monarch*, a former Belfast–Liverpool cross-channel passenger ship and set sail for 'somewhere'. As it was a fairly fast ship we sailed without escort, a host of eager RAF recruits living in comfortable crowded cabins and enjoying meals served in three sittings. The weather was moderately rough, so many meals did not find a permanent home, being disgorged over the side for the benefit of the birds and the fish. Three days later 'somewhere' turned out to be Reykjavik, in Iceland. We were heading for Canada but there was to be a stop for sixteen days at a camp at Alafoss, a small village about ten miles from the Icelandic capital.

Being August it was a very pleasant stay – temperatures 50°F to 60°F. Our days were spent idling, exploring and bathing in a nearby hot spring, the waters of which were channelled off to heat the buildings in Reykjavik – a very pleasant 85°F swim whilst enjoying a distant view of the snow-covered volcano Heckla.

Socially, there was not much to do in Iceland. The landscape consisted of rocks and more rocks, with some grass growing through close to the sea shores. The Nissen huts were very basic in furnishings except for a pot stove and bare boards on which to sleep. It was necessary to turn over frequently so that the pain on one side of the body matched the ache on the other side. Daylight was about twenty hours per day.

The best one could say about the local inhabitants was that they 'tholed' us. We were treated as an occupying army (which we were) and left to get on with being unwanted. A mate and I did make contact with two young ladies whilst out on an exploratory walk. They were pleasant, but distant, and made themselves scarce once we reached the outskirts of habitations. Our ideas of a pleasant social life, including dances and flirting, had to be firmly revised.

We were beginning to feel that we were forgotten when, without prior notice, word came to pack up and head back to Reykjavik where the former Canadian Pacific passenger liner the *Montcalm*, now HMS *Wolf*, was prepared to provide us with passage to Canada. The *Montcalm* was operating as an armed merchant cruiser giving escort coverage to convoys. As a result, when we set sail we travelled southeast to the north coast of Ireland to collect a convoy before turning west towards our destination of Halifax. The ship provided my first experience of sleeping in a hammock – very comfortable for a time, until I tried to turn, when falling out was easier to accomplish.

Fortunately the passage to Halifax was uneventful and we arrived there one evening to find the lights of the city shining down before us, just like Fairyland. Indeed that was how life in Canada remained, for all of us who had experienced the blackouts, rationing and, perhaps, the blitzes of wartime Britain.

The following morning we disembarked, marched to the railway station and climbed aboard a Canadian National train bound for Charlottetown, Prince Edward Island. I say 'climbed aboard' as it was my first experience of getting onto a train which had several steps up from the station platform. Our destination, No 31 Air Navigation School, was a well organised camp at an airfield about two miles outside the town. It was to be our home for nearly four months.

The training was intense – lectures, drill and physical training during the day, followed by flying training exercises, often at night. The aircraft were all Avro Ansons, flown, for the most part, by recently trained pilots with quite limited experience. Whilst we were being trained as navigators, we were encouraged to learn to fly and to make use of the ground based Link Trainer. I did so on a number of occasions until once, when all alone, I got into a spin which I completely failed to correct. With the machine going round and round, I managed to climb out and was very thankful to reach terra firma. As they say in the Air Force, the more 'firma' the less 'terra'.

Charlottetown ice rink in September 1941 with Messrs Rae, Cleworth, Hornby, Sims, Lawson, Roberts, Heath, Barr, Lewis, Hawkins and Pirnie. That's me on the left, giving the 'V' sign!

Most of our navigational exercises were flown over the Northumberland Strait, lying to the south of Prince Edward Island, and would last for two to three hours. We were expected to make landfalls at two locations some 100 miles apart before returning to base. Gradually our map reading improved and that in turn helped us to determine wind force and directions, the vital elements in Dead Reckoning Navigation. We received, and learnt how to use, a sextant, which in turn made us study and identify stars that were helpful for astronavigation and astrofixes. These also required an accurate watch and a time check before takeoff. Attention, too, had to be paid to the aircraft and its compass. Deviation and variation had to be known and calculated. The former corrected the Compass North reading to the true North, whilst the latter corrected for any outside magnetic influences on the compass. It was rather complicated, but without these corrections your actual heading might be wrong by even five to ten degrees, fatal for some.

No 31 Course, 32 ANS at Chalottetown, September 1941

As the training and the course continued we began to appreciate the importance of accurate navigation and to realise that our future, and that of the crew, would depend on our knowledge and ability. Whilst I found flying exciting at first, it soon became routine, and eventually turned out to be a rather uncomfortable way of doing a very necessary job. Perhaps, if I had been a pilot I would have felt differently.

The Avro Anson was by no means the most uncomfortable aircraft that I was to fly in. Its safety record was excellent and any air turbulence caused only minor tummy upsets. One drawback was the undercarriage, which had to be raised and lowered manually. The pilot could do this, but it was normally delegated to a member of the crew. One of my fellow pupils calculated that it took some 200 turns of the handle for each operation. I think I just found it too tiring to check that statistic.

Fortunately during this part of our training accidents were few, but we did lose one crew. A night flight took off for an exercise over the Gulf of St Lawrence and failed to return. It happened towards the end of our course and we never learned what had occurred. I think that it was probably engine failure and a ditching in the sea with all being lost. Whilst the authorities in charge handled such matters with all due respect, I believe that in order to maintain a high morale among the aircrew we were kept in some ignorance of the outcome.

It was very pleasant to be stationed in Charlottetown. The people were most friendly and hospitable and, as we were there for a much longer period, it was possible to learn other people's names. Time off was spent very happily at cinemas, dance halls, cafés, church halls or travelling elsewhere on the Island, often to some wonderful beaches. That was during the early months of our course. Later on there was plenty of frost and snow to curtail some of these activities and eliminate our summer suntans.

By January 1942 our navigation course was complete, and we were judged to be 'satisfactory' navigators. Inwardly I think we all felt somewhat inadequate, as we realised that our training had been under ideal conditions – no blackouts, well forecast weather

Christmas Eve 1941 saw me at the Canadian Legion, Charlottetown. Alec Pirnie and Wally Heath are on the steps.

conditions and a relatively flat countryside. The navigator's worst scenario remained, "If I descend through this cloud will it have a hard centre?"

Leaving Prince Edward Island we now, strangely enough, headed for Prince Edward County, bordering Lake Ontario, our destination being Picton, a small town on the edge of the lake with its adjoining Royal Canadian Air Force (RCAF) station. It was a 36 hour journey by train in the middle of winter, icicles hanging from the Pullman carriages and very comfortable sleeping accommodation. There was a similarity to scenes in the later movie *Some like it hot*, with Jack Lemmon and Marilyn Monroe climbing in and out of bunks. We did the same but no Marilyn Monroes were to be found.

Picton was a bombing and gunnery school with the flying carried out in Fairey Battle aircraft. In these machines the pilot sat in a canopy covered cockpit behind the powerful Rolls Royce engine, whilst the trainee was in an open cockpit to the rear. For bombing practice there was an open hatch on the floor providing good target visibility and of course a bombsight. The cockpit was also fitted with a Vickers machine gun which was operated by the pupil in a standing position. All the exercises were carried out over Lake Ontario, with another aircraft towing a target drogue for gunnery practice and a buoy in the water which we tried to hit with our practice bombs. There was nothing too unusual about all of this except that it was January/February, the temperature hovering around 0°F, and us in an open cockpit peering into a slipstream of perhaps 140 mph! Yes it was cold, but no one on the course had any problem with it and most found the exercises to be fun in a competitive way. There were also lectures, parades and PT to keep us busy. It was an enjoyable course with some 48 hour passes, when we headed for the city of Toronto about 120 miles away. This is not far in Canadian terms, just a pleasant train journey. On one leave I recorded a temperature of -30°F whilst waiting for the train on the platform at Belleville. That and plenty of snow made us thankful for the central heating enjoyed almost everywhere.

Almost all of us had some people to visit in Toronto. Much of the emigration to Toronto had been from Northern Ireland and my contacts were the Haire family, formerly of Cullybackey, then living in High Park Avenue and Quebec Avenue, both in the west of the city. The welcome and hospitality was second to none.

In February 1942 we were pronounced efficient in Bombing and Gunnery. A 'Wings Parade' was held at which an Observer 'O' badge was pinned to our chests and we were all promoted to the rank of Sergeant. A busy evening followed as we sewed the badges and stripes to our best uniforms. Most of us had become quite proficient at needlework during our service and I prided myself on being a 'darn good sock darner'. An 'O' on your chest was much better than two 'O's in your socks!

We were all granted a few days leave and my Scots pal, Jimmy Lawson, and I set off for Boston. Why we went there, where we stayed, and what we did escape me. It is my memory which is faulty, as I am willing to swear that the demon drink was not to blame. Indeed we continued to be as teetotal as all day coffee drinkers.

Returning to Picton after our leave I was surprised and pleased to learn that I and five others in the course were being commissioned – so much for our work sewing on badges and stripes, now it was to be a new uniform with the Pilot Officer's stripe and Observer badge included. Also we did not realise it but this was the beginning of the drifting apart of the graduating members who had been together for about nine months.

Our stay in Canada was coming to an end. We travelled by train and Pullman sleeper to Moncton where the powers that be organised our return to the UK. Moncton was a small town with a very large transit camp; trainees arriving mostly from Britain, and the trained – Canadians and others – going overseas. I cannot remember doing any work or having any lectures, so it was a life of idleness, broken only by our search for the local welfare organisations. These were usually to be found in public halls or churches where tea or coffee and buns were provided whilst we enjoyed concerts, singsongs or dances. Nowhere was the 'evil drink' to be seen partly because of Canada's rather strict liquor laws but also because many of us were almost teetotal, myself included. The young ladies of Moncton must have had a ball with hordes of young men eager to meet them being replaced by more and more other young men with similar desires.

Ten days of that kind of life was evidently considered to be enough and so we were packed on a train and sent on our way. In my case it was to be to Halifax, Nova Scotia where I boarded the SS *Bayano* and from where it set off to cross the Atlantic. We were part of a 6 knot convoy in this Elder and Fyffe banana boat of about 4000 tons. There were about 20 of us accommodated very comfortably in bunk beds, but, oh boy, was it boring. The journey took sixteen days most of which time was spent in our bunks sleeping, reading or overcoming seasickness. Looking back, I shudder to realise what a foolish boy I was. Every night I went to bed in my pyjamas instead of dressing to suit what would have been more appropriate for a day or two in an open lifeboat. Fortunately that dreadful scenario was not to be. The journey was entirely uneventful and not a ship was lost.

It was 17 March 1942 (St Patrick's Day) when we sailed into Liverpool. Next day we travelled by train to London and on to

Bournemouth where I was allotted a ground floor bedroom in the Royal Bath Hotel – most definitely five star! Perhaps cynically, one might say we were like turkeys being fattened for Christmas, but that thought never occurred to us. In the services you learned to make the best of everything and that included making the best of the best. It was to be a four week stay including a leave spent in Belfast and many visits to my Uncle John and other relatives who lived in Bournemouth. Uncle John was my mother's eldest brother; he and his wife fussed over me just as my mother would have done and I enjoyed every bit of it.

The next posting was to Harrogate, another holding station for aircrew in training. Again, I had lots of family to visit. My mother's two sisters and another brother and their families lived in Harrogate. Once more I was pampered in every way possible. The

Back in the United Kingdom, I resumed flying, with training exercises over the Irish Sea. This is a view of the Menai Strait, in North Wales, taken in October 1942 from a Fairey Botha. The ship is HMS *Conway*, a training ship not unlike HMS *Victory* in appearance. Bangor Pier is bottom right.

stay in Harrogate lasted for more than a month, during which time I attended a number of lectures and three times as many dances and picture shows. My daughter Julie, who now lives in Richmond, North Yorkshire, will be interested to learn that on 14 May a number of us went to attend Army manoeuvres there. Probably the visit was to the Catterick Camp, but I have no more memories of the visit than that.

From Harrogate we went to West Freugh, near Stranraer, in Scotland and then on to Dumfries. This was an Advanced Flying Unit where we resumed flying training with a number of cross-country exercises, flying low over the Irish Sea. The flying was in Fairey Bothas, a greatly under powered aircraft which shuddered every bit of the way. Each trip was a white knuckle ride. Not many Bothas were produced and to the best of my knowledge they were never used on operations.

The end of June brought a posting to No 10 Operational Training Unit (OTU) at Abingdon, Oxfordshire and from there to the satellite airfield at Stanton Harcourt. Here we were encouraged to form crews, partly voluntary and partly compulsory. I became part of a five man crew headed by P/O E Hinchcliffe, a tall brawny Canadian. We were to fly Whitley bombers.

For the next couple of months we trained as a crew, going on cross-country flights, practising takeoffs and landings (commonly referred to as circuits and bumps) and spending our free evenings visiting Oxford and other places in the vicinity. It was a peaceful, ordered existence interrupted only by minor occurrences such as a non-serious taxiing accident on 9 August and being confined to camp for going into Oxford when night flying was scheduled; it was a very wet night and we had gambled that flying would be scrubbed. We were wrong!

Then on 6 September a much more serious event occurred. That evening we set off from Oxford on a cross-country exercise which was to take us up to Perth in Scotland and back. Having been in the air for about five hours, and over southeast Scotland, we saw an airfield below with all its landing lights on. The pilot made the

Ed Hinchcliffe, Harry Cheasman, Curt Curtis and Robert (Darkie) Laws pose in front of our Whitley aircraft at Stanton Harcourt in August 1942. Harry Cheasman was killed in action during February 1943. I took the photograph as fifth member of the crew.

decision to land, whether because he was tired or because of engine trouble I know not. We did land but it was about 200 yards short of the runway, in a dense but fairly young forest. I had been sitting on the step beside the pilot which led down to the nose of the aircraft and, as was the custom, I was not strapped in. The Whitley cut the tops off many trees, but none hit the nose and amid much noise we came to rest in complete darkness. I had been thrown head over heels down into the nose of the aircraft, but fortunately I found I was none the worse and was able to pick myself up whilst mentally saying, "Mother, what do I do now?" There were branches of trees all over the aircraft and we were unable to decide whether we were near the ground or perched high up in the trees. The escape hatch over the pilot was clear of debris and cautiously we clambered out and onto one of the wings. Still not knowing how far above the ground we were, I found a tree trunk and slid down it to good old terra firma. Meanwhile in the distance we could hear voices calling out, "Keep shouting, keep shouting, we'll find you!, we'll find you!"

The poor old Whitley was a write-off, but all of us were quite unscathed, except for the pilot who had broken his wrist – a most remarkable result, due in part to the low landing speed of the Whitley and the lack of any fire developing. Praise be!

This was Charterhall, an airfield near Berwick upon Tweed. The personnel there were very kind and efficient in dealing with these strangers from above. We were given medical examinations, debriefed, fed and put to bed. Next day they put us on a train and back we went to Stanton Harcourt. That is, all of us except the pilot who was kept in hospital with his broken wrist. None of us were ever to see him again. The Board of Enquiry into the crash ruled that the cause was engine failure. We were left to think what we liked about that, as the Board did not approach us again.

Possibly because we were no longer a crew, things began to happen. On 8 September we were told that the four remaining were going to be posted to No 102 Squadron at Pocklington. Obviously, we were going as individuals to fly with any crew which was short a member. I had done most of my recent training as Bomb Aimer and so it was to continue. Occasionally I flew with the others, but not on a regular basis.

Two days later and still at OTU flying Whitleys, we learned that that night we would be flying for real. All of the OTU aircraft were required that night for a maximum effort against Dusseldorf – a thousand bomber raid and my first operation. I'm certain I was very apprehensive although the next day I recorded in my diary that I "did not feel too bad, scared a bit at times" and that meant it was "not as bad as expected".

Operation No 2 followed three days later. On all three days we were briefed, but flying was scrubbed on the first two days and on the third day we went to Bremen. After that raid I got a week's leave. It was spent in Belfast and its vicinity. My 1932 Riley car was put on the road to use up the coupon for the five gallons of petrol allotted to me as one who was on operations – a nice perk. I am not sure whether it was on this leave or a later one that I parked the car two nights running outside a dance hall in Causeway Street, Portrush. Emerging on the second night I found two policemen waiting at the car. At the time there was no petrol ration for private use, so no doubt some nearby observer had squealed on me. I think that the police were a little sorry to find that I was not a 'spiv'. However, my explanation and leave passes were accepted and I drove off in the blackout to wherever I was staying.

Returning from leave I reported to No 102 Squadron of No 4 Group Bomber Command at Pocklington, Yorkshire. So began my seven month attachment to an operational squadron flying four-engined Halifax Bombers, a fine aircraft with a performance almost as good as the legendary Lancasters.

Life on the Squadron was made as pleasant as possible; the accommodation was in single or double rooms in Nissen huts. The messes provided very good meals and the opportunity to have a beer or two before and after dining. When operations were not on, passes were freely granted so that we were able to visit York, Harrogate, Hull and all the cafés and dance halls therein. The local lasses never had it so good! Our days were filled with flying exercises, swinging of compasses, checking equipment and lectures of one sort or another. Then there were briefings for operations. For every operation flown we were briefed on average about three times, meaning that two trips were scrubbed (that is cancelled) usually due to weather conditions. All during the day there was much speculation by aircrew of what the weather was likely to be. When a scrub was announced there was considerable satisfaction, if not downright joy. "Let's hit Betty's Bar in York (often referred to as the Briefing Rooms) for a couple of well-watered pints" was the cry and that we did.

However while an operation remained 'On', we were kept at 'action stations', so to speak, all day. The aircraft had to be armed with the required bomb load, ammunition for the guns and otherwise fully checked. Then there were met briefings, combined with the navigation and route information giving wind direction, and speed estimates and cloud cover. The target was named and information given about the defences in the area, the bomb dropping zone and whether it would be marked or not by Pathfinder aircraft. A busy and apprehensive day it was, with a meal served shortly before take off, then a short walk to the flight office, collect a parachute, climb aboard a bus or transport and out to the aircraft to run up the engines ready to go. Each member of the crew also carried his own accessories plus a wide array of items – flasks of tea, pills, eatables, Teddy Bears, good luck charms and in my case my own shoes, worn inside my flying boots, plus what I will refer to as my urine container, more often called a 'piss tin'. From my position in the nose of the aircraft it could be a slow oxygen-free trip to the convenience in the body of the aircraft, hence on long trips the tin was much used. On one occasion, when returning to base my tin was overflowing and in danger of being spilt. Beside me was the escape hatch which I opened gently and poured the contents through the aperture. At the same time, and quite naturally, a gale of slipstream came through the hatch. All was well for about ten minutes, until the pilot called me on the intercom saying, "What did you do with the contents of your tin?" I told him, whereupon he responded somewhat testily, "You so and so, I can taste it!"

It was not until 6 November 1942 that I went on my third Operation – a mine laying operation off the Dutch coast. A Sergeant Barker was the pilot of a scratch crew. Op No 4 followed nine days later. It was a very long trip to Genoa, from which we returned on three engines to land at Tangmere on the south coast, that being the nearest available airfield. Two days later we flew back to Pocklington only to take off the following day for Turin – Op No 5. Again it was a long trip, especially as we were routed in and out by the English Channel, thereby avoiding flying over Germany and the Low Countries. Once more we developed engine trouble just before reaching the Alps, one propeller was feathered, our bombs were jettisoned and we turned to land once again at Tangmere. This time we were ordered to stay there until the aircraft was fixed. That took seven days, during which time I took the opportunity to visit my relatives in Bournemouth and dance halls in Brighton. The ordinary shoes which I wore inside my oversized flying boots came into their own. Always having to wear flying boots was detrimental to an enjoyable social life!

At the end of November I had another fourteen day leave before returning to Pocklington. The Christmas New Year period was very quiet for us, probably because the weather was not favourable for operations – a state welcomed by most of the crews – even the really keen types. Early in January 1943 my sixth operation was a mine laying operation in the Kattegat Sea, north and east of Denmark, seemingly an easy operation as there was not much flying over enemy territory. The Royal Navy demanded considerable accuracy in dropping the mines which were intended to destroy shipping from Sweden and Norway. As a consequence we flew somewhat lower over Denmark in order to obtain visual fixes of our position. This resulted in considerable small arms ack-ack fire; it was tracer coming up towards us, very slow at first, then faster until it flew past at lightning speed – not a pretty sight and more than a little scary. Fortunately for us the gunners' aims were a little off. On 17 January we went to Berlin, an operation which I well remember, because we avoided nose to nose contact with a Lancaster by about 20 feet when over the target. The flight lasted eight hours and we landed at Coltishall, Norfolk with a few small shell holes in the fuselage. Operations 8 and 9 followed with the targets Lorient and St Nazaire. These were attempts to try to help the battle against the U-boats.

In February I contracted a bad cold which was made worse by an outbreak of shingles at the same time. A number of nights had to be spent in the sickbay trying not to scratch my right side too energetically. The cause was not disclosed by the doctor, but probably it was stress, a condition to which we remained oblivious.

Bale Out!

Feeling better, I was included in a crew for Hamburg on 3 March but as the pilot, Warrant Officer Lewis, took sick, we jettisoned our bombs once again, and returned to base. It was a sad finale for the pilot who went into hospital and off operations.

There followed another two weeks leave in Belfast, and on return Flt Lt Milne and I were sent to Morecambe to take part in a fundraising campaign, or as it was referred to – a 'Line Shooting Bash'. Back to reality at Pocklington I was crewed up with Wally 'Lash' Lashbrook for the first time. He was returning to start a second tour of operations after being an Instructor at a Conversion Flight – changing two-engine pilots into four-engine pilots. The target for operation number 11 was Stuttgart, a very long trip, almost all of it over Germany. However it all went off well, except for being coned by searchlights near the target. This was always a frightening experience, you felt that every ack-ack gun within miles was trained upon you, and very often they were.

Two days later, on 16 April 1943, we were briefed to go to the Skoda works at Pilsen, Czechoslovakia. This would normally have been a long trip but it would be an extra long one for me!

Opposite: Some officers of No 102 Squadron outside their mess at Pocklington in April 1943. Ken Bolton of our crew is on the extreme right, I'm in the centre, at the back, and the others include Flt Lt Milne, Sqn Ldr Marshall, F/O Jimmy Hinchcliffe, Wg Cdr Coventry, F/O McDonald, F/O Haines and Sqn Ldr Marchbank.

Chapter 2:
The middle, and all is not so well
(The events of 1943 as recollected and written in 1944.)

It was 16 April and, as usual, we heard early in the morning that we were operating that night. Little did I realise that this time it was going to be entirely different from the previous 11 trips which I had made. All of those trips, including Berlin, Bremen, Dusseldorf, Stuttgart, St Nazaire and Genoa, had been very successful. Never had we been very hard pushed, although once we had some slight damage by flak, and on two occasions we returned on three engines. My first two trips had been made in Whitley aircraft and the remainder in Halifaxes.

The crew of which I was the Bomb Aimer comprised: 'Lash', the pilot; Ken Bolton, the navigator; 'Nippy' Knight, the engineer; 'Darky', Bob Laws, the wireless operator; 'Laurie' the mid-upper gunner; and Willie, the rear gunner. Of these 'Lash', Ken and Willie were all very experienced, having just come back to carry out their second tour of operations: so that all of them had about thirty trips to their credit. The rest of us each had about the same number of trips, and having been separated from our original crews at some time or other a new crew was formed and this was to be our second trip together.

Well, as I have already said, news came through early in the morning, and of course, the usual rush started – visiting the aircraft, 'T' Tommy, testing our equipment, chatting with the ground crew, and also making sure that we had all our necessary kit. Briefing took place about 4.00pm, and we learned that the target was to be the Skoda Works at Pilsen, Czechoslovakia. It was a long trip, much longer than any of the others which I had done, as in order to avoid defences we were routed to fly to the south coast of England, and from there across France, Belgium, and southern Germany to the target. The distance was approximately 2,000 miles, which meant about ten hours flying, of which time about six hours would be spent over enemy territory. The route was rather close to heavily defended areas like Mannheim, Frankfurt, and Nuremberg, so that it was not an operation which we fancied instinctively. Still, the boys took it with the usual complacency, and all looked forward to being able to add a new place name to their list. Having been briefed for weather, enemy opposition, times to attack, and so forth, we all collected our 'Escape Aids' and went to the mess, where a meal was waiting. After eating, flying clothes were donned, thence to the flights where the crews collected and so out to the aircraft for that final check before starting up the engines.

Takeoff was about half an hour before darkness, and at 8.40pm we were airborne. Five minutes later we set course for the south coast of England. The trip to the target was quiet, with just a few searchlights in different places and not much flak; halfway there we saw one plane shot down in flames, but that was all there was to show that fighters were around. At the target we descended to 4,000 feet for bombing, having flown out at around 10,000 feet. The first time across the area we were unable to identify the factory buildings, so we circled round and came in again on the same heading, and this time we got rid of the load – all High Explosive bombs. The defences were not very heavy, but several bursts must have been fairly close as we could hear them and they shook the aircraft. The time of bombing was approximately 1.50am.

Having left the target area, we set course for home, and again things were quiet with some slight searchlight and ack-ack activity in the region of Frankfurt. Up to this time the weather had been clear but an hour or so after bombing we ran into some clouds. One of these caused rather severe ice to form on the aircraft, and we had to climb speedily to 14,000 feet in order to get clear.

After a short time the cloud disappeared and we again descended to about 10,000 feet. The weather was very fine now and an almost full moon gave excellent visibility. Things proceeded very quietly for some time, but when we saw three aircraft being shot down in flames within a few minutes of each other we knew that fighters were near. The skipper immediately told our rear gunner, Willie, to keep an extra special lookout, and we continued our gentle weaving for about two minutes until suddenly there was a loud swish and at the same time the sound of bullets ripping into the fuselage.

A moment's silence, then the skipper's voice over the intercom: "Anyone hurt?" I replied, "OK here, Skip", the navigator's okay followed, and then Willie with, "All fine, Skip, I didn't see the blighter", to which the Skipper replied, "OK, I am going into a steep turn, keep your eyes skinned in case they come in again."

After another fraction of a second the skipper said, "Port inner engine on fire." I looked out and saw that the flames were burning all around it and back over the wing for about six feet; they were blue in the slipstream just like the flame from a blow-torch. It looked anything but healthy! Another very brief silence followed, then, "Prepare to abandon aircraft" came from the Skipper, which order I acknowledged before getting into action. I attached my parachute to the harness which I was wearing, turned round in the nose, and started assisting Ken to get clear of the floor escape hatch, as normally his chair folded down on top of it. To me he seemed very slow in stepping clear, but it must have been only a fraction of a second until I had my hand on the handle and was pulling open the door. It opened inwards, coming off its hinges when it came to the vertical so that it could be jettisoned out through the opening. I did this, but unfortunately the slipstream caused it to jam edgeways and diagonally across the escape exit. Frantically I tried to kick it clear, but it was held at the side distant from me and I could not reach across the opening with sufficient strength to free it. I tried to gesticulate to Ken what was required, but he did not understand. Then came the final order, more in the nature of a plea, "Bale out for ****'s sake, before the wing blows off" and I could wait no longer. Quickly disconnecting my oxygen and intercom, I jumped upon the edge of the door, and next moment found myself floating in space.

My first impression was a fleeting glimpse of the black tail against the starry sky. There was no somersaulting and I could feel myself in a sitting position. Immediately I grasped the handle of my parachute and pulled. It came away and, very slowly it seemed, I felt the cords and silk of the 'chute pass over my head. At last it was fully open and I could see the large white circle above my head; I was swinging violently, and had to steady myself by pulling on the cords.

My thoughts during the descent were very varied. First I felt very thankful in being safely out of the aircraft, even though I was dangling in space. Then I wondered about my companions, and tried to turn around to see if there were any other parachutes visible, but I could not get myself turned and all I could see over my shoulder was the plane burning on the ground. I felt very doubtful about their safety, as from the time we were hit until the plane was burning on the ground cannot have been more than four or five minutes. We were flying at about 9,000 feet when we were hit and, as we had lost height very quickly, I calculated that I must have got out at about 5,000 feet, which did not leave much time for the rest of the crew. Still I continued to descend, although I appeared to be almost motionless and there was no sensation of falling.

I looked at my watch by the light of the moon: it was five minutes past four. Then I fell to wondering where and how I would fall. I had a look down and saw that the district was thickly wooded, and I imagined myself hanging from a tree for days. However, I was drifting with the wind, and as I got lower I saw that I was going to be lucky and have a field for my fall; there were plenty of trees nearby, and a small cottage, but the field was for me.

Until the last one hundred feet I seemed to fall very slowly and barely noticed the objects getting bigger, but then the earth seemed to rush up to meet me and I hit the ground heavily. As I had my face into the wind, my parachute pulled me and I rolled over on my back, which helped me to take the shock of the fall. Immediately I was on my feet again, in time to see the silk flutter to the ground, and also to see that I had missed a barbed wire fence by a few feet.

There was a profound stillness everywhere, made much more noticeable after the noise of engines which I had been hearing up to a few minutes before. However, there was no time to lose as it wanted but two hours to daylight and somehow I had the feeling that Germans would pounce on me any minute.

The field in which I found myself was surrounded on two sides by woods, with the cottage about 100 yards away. My first job was to hide my parachute so I had a quick look around and I discovered a drinking pond for cattle in one corner of the field.

Our mid upper Gunner in HR 663 was Sergeant Laurie Neill, who hailed from Bradford. Laurie survived the crash and was taken prisoner by the Germans. This picture was taken in April 1943.

Here I was able to push my parachute and Mae West down into the mud. Never before had I realised that they were so big. They just refused to go out of sight and I was too excited and too frantic to make a thorough job of it. However I got them covered sufficiently to escape a casual glance. Then I started to half run and half walk; first I skirted the cottage and then set off in a northerly direction, taking my bearings from the moon and stars. I had wanted to go west, but as I could see the glow from the burning plane in that direction, it would have been dangerous to do so. Obviously the Germans would go to the aircraft first and then start searching from there; my position was about two miles from the crash.

For perhaps half an hour I walked through the fields until I came to a wood where I rested a few minutes and altered my clothing so that my heavy white flying sweater was underneath my shirt. I put on my collar and tie, and cut all the identification marks, such as the wings and epaulettes, off my battle dress tunic. At the same time I smoked half a cigarette from the few which I had in my pocket, making sure that the flame from the match would not show in the darkness. The smoke was wonderful, and helped to steady my nerves. Continuing to walk, I kept going through the wood for about half an hour until I came to the edge when I decided to skirt its borders in a northwesterly direction. It was now becoming light and I did not want to get into the open too much for if I were discovered it would be possible to run into the wood.

Walking along the edge I came across a section which had been cleared of trees, and logs were stacked here and there. Apparently woodcutters had been working here recently, as I discovered a very old and dirty black cotton coat which I put on over my battle dress tunic to help my disguise. Having skirted the trees for some distance, at last I could walk beside the wood no longer without going south, so I again cut across the fields and over a road. I continued walking until 6.30am, when it was so light that I decided I would have to find a hiding place. I chose a sort of disused path, which had hedges on either side and brambles in the middle. It suited my purpose as I had a fairly good view all round; the cover could have been better and I might have found a place more suitable but I did not wish to remain in the open any longer.

Now I had time to examine myself and found that I had two rather nasty cuts on my hands and one on my left ear. I had not the least idea how I had got them but luckily they were not very serious. However, they were very dirty and I washed them in a cattle pond which was nearby. At the same time I filled the rubber water bottle out of my escape kit and put in a pill specially supplied for decontaminating water. The kit also contained a bar of chocolate, Horlicks tablets, some chewing gum, a tube of condensed milk, needles and thread, a compass, matches, tablets to counteract fatigue, a file, 2000 francs in French money, and maps covering almost all of the Continent. It was breakfast time by now and although I was very hungry I had to be content with nibbling at a square of chocolate, a couple of Horlicks tablets and a drink of water, finishing off with the other half of the cigarette which I smoked until it burned my lips.

Time passed slowly. I could see and hear people in the fields but no one came near me. There was an old woman milking some cows, a man and a boy driving cattle and also a few cyclists on the road about 200 yards away, all going about their everyday business. It seemed so unreal to me in my hiding place. I did not know exactly what I expected but I still had the feeling that they were just waiting for me to show myself and then I would be captured. These people were doing the same as they did the day before, whereas with me things were so different.

The sun came up beautifully warm in an almost cloudless sky, and its heat warmed me so much that I began to feel drowsy in spite of my excitement. To keep me off the damp earth I lay down on my flying boots, which I had been wearing up to this time. Luckily I had worn my ordinary shoes inside my flying boots otherwise my feet might have suffered from the walking.

I dozed fitfully, perhaps for ten or fifteen minutes at a stretch, wakening up every now and then to look around or to discover the source of any unexpected noise. About 1.00pm, when I was still dozing, I heard sounds of something beating against bushes. Immediately I was fully awake but could not discover the origin of the noise, although I knew that it was not far away. It appeared to come from down the path in which I was hiding, but sounded too violent to be made by a human being. I hid as well as possible, but the sound came nearer and, suddenly, a cow appeared, coming towards me up the path with a boy behind driving it along. Evidently the cow had broken out of a field and was being chased by the boy. It emerged so suddenly that I was taken aback and had to stand up to keep out of its way. Mentally I cursed it, but it was too late – the boy had seen me. He paused. We looked each other up and down. Then, wonder of wonders, he put his hand to his cap in way of a salute. I could almost have cried; there was a lump in my throat and I could not speak. I gulped, and touched my bare head with my hand in response to his welcome. He came up to me and we shook hands; still I could not speak. I was so overcome I could not concentrate my thoughts. Besides, he would not understand English, and momentarily I seemed to forget every French word I had known. But how had he recognised me? I was no longer dressed very like an airman: he certainly was very quick. Even now I do not know how he understood, although I have been told that I do look typically British; perhaps he had heard about the plane crashing in the neighbourhood.

After several minutes I managed a few French words, which he understood. I explained that I was a British airman and that I had come down by parachute during the night. It was not easy and I had to gesticulate with my hands though it was even harder for me to understand his questions. However we managed somehow: he asked about my clothes, my companions, in what direction the aircraft lay, where my parachute and flying kit were, what was my name, my age, and where did I live. Then he asked if I was hungry and when I said "Yes" and showed him the little that I had, he said he would go but would return with something to eat.

We had talked for about half an hour; all the time in undertones, and now he crept away leaving me once more on my own. He had told we that his name was André, that he was 12 years of age and that he worked on a farm with his father and brother. His friendliness had touched me and his manner showed the sympathy for our cause, which he held along with many of the other people of these occupied countries.

It was not long before he came back with some cold potatoes in a pot and a large bottle of beer. Both were very welcome and tasted as good as anything I had ever had. During the afternoon and evening he visited me several times, and once brought his father and brother with whom I talked. An elderly woman also came to the hiding place and brought me some bread and cheese and a couple of hard boiled eggs. Apparently she was a friend of André's father. We could not understand each other, but in parting she shook my hand and kissed me on both cheeks.

To André and his father I showed my maps and asked where I was. The maps were not very detailed and they could not give the exact position, but I made out that I was near a village called Sivry, on the borders of France and Belgium. In fact I must have crossed the border during my walk of the previous night, as they pointed it out to me – not more than a mile away. I told them that I intended to start walking again when it got dark, and they said that if I went to the village of Soire le Chateau, about four miles due west, I might be able to get help. Their instructions were quite comprehensive but I had difficulty in understanding what they meant. They were dissatisfied with my clothes, and brought me an old grey coat and a light brown cap, which certainly helped my disguise. In exchange I gave them my flying boots and my battle dress tunic, also a couple of English coins as souvenirs. They refused to take any French money from me, saying that I would need it later to buy food. On a piece of paper they wrote out their address and gave it to me, but when they had left I tore it into small pieces and buried it. It would have been very dangerous for them if the Germans had caught me with their address.

About 8.00pm they went away, leaving me another package of food for my journey. They were very good and regretted that it was not within their power to help me further. I hoped that after the war I would be able to meet them again, safe, well, and happy. (I did so in 1976, more of which later.)

About 10.30pm it was sufficiently dark for me to start walking so I set off due west as arranged. All the time I kept to the fields, crossing the roads as quickly as possible. Sometimes the hedges were very thick and I had to walk halfway round a field until I could find

This is Major Wilhelm Herget who commanded I/NJG/4 at Florennes, Belgium. According to Belgian historian, Dr Tommy de Tournay, on the night of 17 April 1943, Herget, flying a Messerschmitt Me 110, shot down a Lancaster and a Halifax returning from Pilsen; the Halifax was HR 663 from No 102 Squadron, my aircraft! HR 663 crashed at Epsauvage, Belgium on the land of the chateau belonging to Dr de Tournay.

When I landed I hid in a disused laneway, with a good all round view. I kept dozing off as the sun warmed the day but about one o'clock I was disturbed by the noise of something in the bushes; it was a cow being chased by a young boy. That young boy, seen here some years later, was 12 year old André Leleu, from Sivry, on the French-Belgian border. André and his father brought me food and gave me directions to a place where I might find help.

Bale Out!

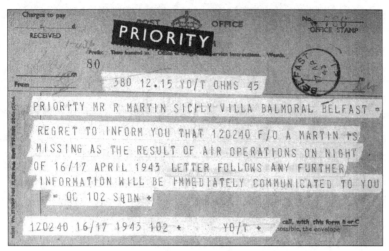

The telegram to my father from the Officer Commanding No 102 Squadron informing him that I was missing in action.

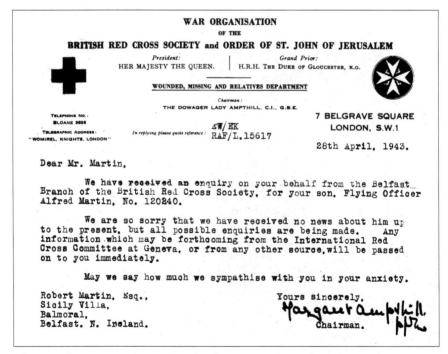

The British Red Cross Society and the Order of St John attempted to keep families informed about missing relatives.

a place to clamber through, so that my course was very erratic. Some of the fields were ploughed which made for very heavy walking, but most were pastures; in these there were plenty of cows, which looked and sounded very eerie at times. I had to keep well clear of farmhouses as I found that they all possessed dogs which barked if I came too close – also I had no desire to be bitten. After the warm day it was very cold and there was a heavy dew on the grass so that I got my feet and legs wet. My feet squelched in my shoes, and I wished very heartily that I had not given away my flying boots.

About midnight I came to Soire le Chateau and made my way round the outskirts. At that hour it was very quiet and uninviting, with only a few lights from badly blacked-out windows. I could not make up my mind whether to knock at a house or not, but once when I was considering it a dog started to bark very loudly and I beat a hasty retreat.

By this time I was feeling rather miserable, so I looked for somewhere to lie down. The first place I tried was the remains of an old chicken house, which comprised a triangular roof lying on some boards. I crawled underneath and dozed for about an hour; but it was too cramped and too cold so I set off to try to find somewhere else. For about an hour I wandered around until I came across a cowshed with three sides and a roof. I hoped to find straw inside but there was none and I lay down on the ground and tried to sleep. As my feet were uncomfortable I took off my wet shoes and socks and wrapped my feet in my cap. Every half hour I had to get up and do exercises to warm myself, and so I passed four hours until it was almost light. Then, as there was a farm nearby, I had to move on. Finding a small clump of bushes I hid there, ate something from my package, and waited until midday, by which time my socks and shoes had been dried by the sun.

It was Sunday and as I had not seen anyone about in the fields I decided to walk to see if I could contact someone who could give me help. I was still fairly close to the village but I preferred the country and so I set off walking south. For about two hours I walked, passing many farms, but I was afraid to go up to any of them. At the end of that time I came to a wood which stretched as far as I could see on either side. There was a road going through it and I decided to walk in the wood close to the road in the hope that I would see someone who looked friendly. After a time I did see two women walking along and decided to approach them. I was a pretty dishevelled sight and they were obviously very frightened when I appeared at the edge of the wood. I made them understand who I was and what I wanted, but they were afraid and although they seemed sympathetic they said they could not help me. In view of this I did not wait long but went back into the wood and put as much distance as possible between them and me.

Again I came into the open and after passing a number of farms I decided to approach one and try my luck. First I had a good look round to make sure that there was no telephone, and then I went up to an old man who was cutting wood. He did not understand me but fetched another man who was evidently the owner of the house. This man was very interested in me and wanted to know all about myself and about the war, but as he made no signs that he was going to help I did not stay with him very long.

At about 6.00pm I had some more food and also washed myself as well as possible in a pond using my handkerchief as a towel. Continuing to walk I crossed a railway and then came to a river which was too wide to jump and too deep to wade so I followed along its banks, until I came to an old rickety rope bridge which I crossed. Nearby there was another farm and after watching it for ten or fifteen minutes and seeing only a woman and a lame hunchbacked man I went up to the house. They were friendly and took me inside, giving me a peculiar kind of tart to eat and some wine. The man also gave me his tobacco and I rolled myself a very rough cigarette, which was none the less very enjoyable. I had the greatest difficulty in making out what they said, and could not get any satisfaction from the answers to my questions. They enquired if I had an identity card and I answered, "No." Then I made enquiries about the railway and asked whether an identity card was necessary to get a ticket. From what I made out the man advised me to travel by a train at 8.00pm, and showed me how to get to the station. He also gave me a map of the district and pointed out exactly where I was; it was a village called Lessies.

I must have been getting careless because I decided to walk past the station and see what it looked like. I had no definite intention of catching the train, but I could not make up my mind what would be best and I was tired wandering about and getting nowhere. Anyway it was a foolish thing to do as it meant walking along roads, and my 'civilian' clothes were not all they might have been. About 7.40pm I arrived at a main road from where I could see the station, with the name written in large letters. I walked down the road, crossed the railway by a level crossing and turned down another road past the station. It was a very small village with this station on the outskirts, and only one or two houses nearby. The only people I saw were sitting on a seat outside what appeared to be an hotel; there were only about four of them but I felt very awkward and obvious as I walked past them trying my best to look natural. However, they did not pay any attention and I walked on, past the entrance to the station, which was closed, and down a hill away from the village.

I did not know what to do and I was still trying to make up my mind when, turning a corner in the road, I saw two gendarmes, both with bicycles, talking to a woman just 50 yards away. My heart nearly stopped, but it was no good turning back as they were looking in my direction, and in any case I did not want to go through the village again. So I walked on, trying to look as unconcerned as possible, although all the time I was quivering inside and hoping they would not pay any attention to me. That 50 yards seemed like miles!

At last I was up to them and just about to pass when one of them said, "Carte d'identite, Monsieur?" They blocked the way, and I had to do something. I started going through my pockets, without saying a word, as if I had lost it – then I made signs that I could not find it. They started asking questions, which I did not understand, so I pointed to my mouth, pretending that I was dumb. They understood that, but continued asking questions which I answered by shaking or nodding my head according to which I thought would be the correct answer to the question. At last they indicated to me to come with them, and the three of us started walking back towards the village.

One of them was small, pleasant faced and the senior of the two, whilst the other was fairly tall and severe. We walked about 30 or 40 yards – both of them looking me up and down. I had just decided to run for it when the small one said, "Anglais?" and after a moment's hesitation I replied, "Oui." We stopped. They talked between themselves for a few minutes, then the smaller one said, "Allez vite" and pointed down the road. I did not wait for any more but turned and started walking as quickly as possible. I had to curb my desire to run, as it would have looked peculiar to the woman who was still watching. Certainly I was very lucky, especially when I think that if I had not acted dumb the woman would have known that I was British, and the gendarmes would have been forced to arrest me, even though they were friendly. It was my biggest fright and I was determined to be more careful in future.

For perhaps a quarter of a mile I had to keep to the road until I was able to enter a wood where I continued walking for some time. While I was in the wood I kept a lookout for some hut or shelter to spend the night, remembering how cold I had been the previous evening. But I came across nothing suitable, and I had almost decided to make myself a bed with dry leaves and twigs when I came upon the railway line again.

There was a road nearby with a level crossing and a gate-keeper's house, and I thought it wiser to cross the line at the crossing rather than anywhere else, where I would look too much like a fugitive. So I made my way out onto the road, and seeing no one near the house, I started to cross the line.

Just as I came opposite the house I noticed a woman in the doorway. I walked on; then changing my mind I retraced my steps and asked in very bad French if she could help me. She was very frightened, and although she understood what I meant, she showed no signs of helping. However I persisted, giving her as much information as I could about myself and answering all her questions.

It was late, about 9.00pm, and I was tired and getting rather desperate. At last I was rewarded as she appeared to trust me. She invited me into the house and there gave me some milk and bread and butter. It was very welcome, and whilst I ate we sat and talked.

Her name was Madame Fernand; she was about 25, and she told me that her husband was interned in Germany. She asked me where I was going to sleep, and when I said that I was going to stay in the wood she said that she would take me to a house where I could spend the night. By this time she seemed friendly enough, and I decided to trust her. So when it was dusk we set off up the road, walking for about a mile until we came to a gate, and then to a farmhouse where we knocked. A man answered the door; Madame spoke to him and we went inside. There was another man in the room, who I thought was a brother of the first although actually he was the farmhand. They scrutinised me very closely, and asked me the usual questions as to where and when I had crashed, what had happened to the remainder of the crew, and so forth.

Apparently I satisfied them as they told me I could stay the night, and they would see what could be done to help me. Later on two women and two children came in; they made me supper and showed me my bed for the night. This was very welcome and it was not long until I was asleep.

Next morning when I got up all the family were at work, milking the cows. They told me that I would have to stay with them for a couple of days until they could arrange for my escape, so I settled down to wait until I could travel once more. At first I hoped to leave within a week, but gradually the time lengthened and it turned out that I did not get away until almost six weeks had elapsed. This period was by no means unpleasant. It was only marred by two things; firstly, I wondered how my parents were keeping, and secondly, I was worried at the thought of being caught in the house with these good people; they would be shot, whilst I would only be taken prisoner.

The family comprised Monsieur and Madame Coolen, Maria, a sister of M Coolen, four children – Lucille, aged 15, Jeanne 13, Leon, 11, and Louise 10 – and lastly René, the farmhand, a lad of only 16, although he looked at least five years older. The two elder children were at school at Fourmies, so I only saw them when they were home for a fortnight over Easter.

Never has anyone been treated better than I was during those six weeks. They did everything in their power to make me as comfortable and happy as possible; all the time I was treated as a guest and I had to insist on being allowed to do odd jobs about the house.

The farm was about two miles from a village called Sains du Nord, and was only small with about a dozen cows, a pair of horses and a few hens and pigs. There was no arable land, except a couple of acres on which they grew their own vegetables. Seldom was I able to go outside the house or yard as I had to hide if anyone came near, so my jobs consisted of peeling potatoes, scraping carrots, washing dishes, helping at the separator after milking or feeding the calves and pigs.

Sometimes, when there was a chance of a search of the farm by the Germans, I would be hidden in a hole deep in the straw in the barn. This was really the home of a recently born calf whose birth had not been disclosed to the authorities and whose future was to be a delicious veal stew. My future in the hiding place was less predictable as it was a rather hot and steamy place with a heavy stench of 'Toujours Manure' in the air.

The wireless was my greatest joy as I was able to listen to the BBC news and once I heard a *Workers' Playtime* programme from a factory at Newforge, two miles from my home. Then I tried to read some French novels, but found them very hard to understand. Altogether the days passed very slowly and it was difficult at times not to feel a bit restless.

The food was good but very plain as the people had to exist largely on what they produced themselves. Breakfast, at 8.30am, usually comprised coffee, black bread, butter, a white creamy soft cheese or black treacle and, sometimes, a boiled egg or a very small piece of ham (very different from ham at home). At 12.30pm there was another meal. This was made up of a very large bowl of vegetable soup and afterwards there was bread, without butter, and a large dish of potatoes served with either turnips or leeks. In addition there might be a small piece of meat, usually ham or some kind of minced meat, while over it all was spread a kind of sauce made from the cream of the milk. We also had cider with this meal,

I was taken to stay with the Coolen family at Sains du Nord while my escape was arranged. The four Coolen children are pictured in this 1947 view.

I spent six weeks with the Coolens, staying in the room beyond M Coolen's car. This picture was taken about 1970.

I was able to visit the Coolen family after the war, my first visit being in 1953. This is the family about 1947, with some of their cattle.

This photograph, taken on 23 July 1967, includes Monsieur Coolen (right), Madame Coolen and their son Leon (beside M Coolen). The other gentlemen are relations.

followed by coffee. The last meal of the day was at 8.30pm after the work was ended and the cows had been milked. It was invariably either warm bread and milk, or soup with bread, butter, treacle, and coffee. Although the coffee was very 'ersatz' and did not taste in the least like real coffee, it was not unpalatable and I got to like it.

On occasions, the late-evening meal was quite liquid, leaving me feeling bloated and in need of that urine container of days gone by. I slept in a front bedroom and because the 'wee house' was some distance from the back door, on awakening during the night with an urgent need for relief, I would go out the front door and 'perform' under my bedroom window. As my only attire was my RAF shirt my appearance would have been quite a ghostly sight to anyone passing on the main road.

Sundays were non-working days (except for the milking). All the family went to church, while in the afternoon René played football. On these days we had wine instead of cider at our midday meal.

Very often people would call at the house, especially on Sundays. Sometimes it was only to collect milk and they did not stay more than a few minutes, but at other times they remained several hours, all of which time I spent in my bedroom in hiding. In the latter weeks I met one or two of these people – those who were more closely connected with the family. Once or twice, too, I remained in the room whilst people were visiting; I was introduced as a brother of M Coolen, and the people were told that I could not speak French. M Coolen had originally come from Belgium and was really Flemish, so this story passed off very well. However, the whole time I was in the company of strangers I felt very uncomfortable and, of course, I could never open my mouth.

All this time I was wondering what would happen to me and I had great difficulty in finding out anything, but as I could do nothing I just had to be patient. Twice M Coolen went off to Lille, evidently to see people, but he seemed uncertain about the whole thing and very cautious. Once I had to fill in a questionnaire with various details about the remainder of my crew, approximately where we had crashed and so forth. Evidently they were checking and I wondered if any of the others from the crew were trying to escape too. I was worried about them, as it did not seem to me that many of them would have had time to parachute to safety. One report did come to me that in a crash in the vicinity of Sivry one person had been killed and the rest had escaped, but I was rather doubtful, as the details did not seem to tally.

The first event of note was a visit on 27 April by a lady schoolteacher from Lille. She was Mme Lagersie, and could speak very good English. I enjoyed the visit tremendously and learnt everything possible about what might happen to me; she acted as interpreter between M Coolen and myself.

Although I was picking up French very quickly it was difficult to understand anything out of the ordinary. Nothing definite could be arranged about my journey but she was going to see if she could find out anything in Lille and get in touch with M Coolen. She, herself, did not know anything about an organisation for people like myself, except that such a thing existed.

Mme Lagersie was very anti-Nazi and wanted to do everything in her power to help. One story she told me was rather amusing. It was about an airman who had baled out over Lille and landed in someone's backyard. He had not had the opportunity to escape but, before being taken away by the Germans, he was the centre of attraction for a queue of women wishing to kiss him on both cheeks.

My next bit of excitement was a visit to the barber in the nearby village. It was 10 May, and my hair had grown very long even though I had tried to cut it myself. M Coolen and I travelled into the village about 8.00pm by the horse and trap. The barber's shop was very small and a one man affair. M Coolen had his hair cut first, then I followed, and again I was passed off as M Coolen's Flemish brother. Although everything went off successfully I was very excited and rather afraid the whole time.

In the fifth week M Coolen got some news though I could not find out exactly what it was. Anyway one evening a lady, Mlle Adele, came up from the village and dyed my hair black. It was rather a joke to me and I wondered what my friends at home would have thought. Having previously been ginger, I doubt If they would have recognised me, and, indeed, I had difficulty

Right: On 27 April 1943 I was visited at the Coolen's by the very anti-Nazi Mme Lagersie. She helped arrange my journey onwards from Sains du Nord.

myself when I looked in a mirror. My eyebrows and eyelashes were darkened also and, really, I looked a villainous sight. The children, Louise and Leon, were amazed at the sight but must have been told not to laugh as they just looked incredulous.

All my clothes were prepared for my departure. My Air Force trousers had been dyed black; I had been given a black coat and a beret, everything to make me look as inconspicuous as possible. They had even supplied me with a false identity card, using the photograph which I had carried with me hidden in my uniform.

On two different days I expected people to call and take me away, but both times I was disappointed. Then, on 26 May, M Dumont and Mme Witton arrived, and I left with them to catch a train at 6.00pm. I was very sorry to say goodbye to the Coolens as they had been exceedingly good to me. I had to promise to visit them after the war. They gave me a wonderful send off; all the family being there to shake my hand and wish me good luck. (As I was living in Canada after the war, my first visit was not until 1953. My sister, Dorothy, and I travelled via Brussels to Sains du Nord where the Coolens, and their friends, gave us a great welcome.)

Bale Out!

M Coolen took the three of us down to the station by the horse and trap, and there we found that the train was two hours late, as the line had been blown up that morning by French patriots. We had to wait in the station for those two hours and I certainly did not feel comfortable, as the first German soldier I had seen was among the crowd. He was walking about and every minute I expected him to come up to me. It was a ridiculous sensation but I just could not help myself. Half an hour of the time was spent in a café drinking beer and, again, I was most uncomfortable with so many strangers in close proximity.

At last the train arrived and we got into a compartment where there were no other travellers. Here I felt more at ease and we were able to talk and eat sandwiches. Due to the delay of the train the plans had to be changed. Originally it had been intended to change trains at Valenciennes and go to Arras, but now, as it was late, M Dumont and Mme Witton decided to travel straight to Lille, stay in an hotel there, then journey to Arras first thing in the morning.

After an uneventful journey the train arrived at Lille about 10.30pm, and we went out into the town in search of an hotel. The town was full of German soldiers and airmen evidently having a night's recreation; the majority were in groups but some were with girls. Nevertheless I imagined that their main occupation was watching me and to cover up I took Mme Witton's arm, and we walked along hoping that we looked like sweethearts. Apparently the Gestapo visited hotels at intervals checking the guests, so it was necessary for us to find a very third class place where we were more likely to pass undetected. It was difficult, and we had to try several places before being successful.

At last we found a suitable place in a side street where we had to fill in some forms giving particulars from our identity cards. Before retiring we had a drink of wine and some bread (for which coupons were given) in the café downstairs, after which the landlady showed us to our rooms. One room was for M and Mme and another, next door, for myself.

The bed looked inviting, and after arranging to get up at 4.00am in order to catch a train I prepared to get into bed. When I was ready I could not find the switch for the electric light. There was a switch behind the bed but it looked more like a bell button and I was afraid that it might summon the landlady, so I decided to take out the light bulb. That was all well and good until about five minutes later when the landlady came up and started knocking next door. She was only looking for a sheet as it happened but when Mme and she came to my door and wanted in I had to get out of bed quickly to open the door. Of course the landlady tried to put on the light with the switch behind the bed and it did not work. Very quickly I had to retrieve the bulb, hop onto the bed and put it back in its socket. All this I did without the landlady suspecting; she only thought that the bulb had been loose, but I felt quite shaken by the affair, especially as I had to act dumb the whole time.

During the night I slept very little, just dozing from time to time and waiting for 4.00am. At last the hour came, I got up, washed, and was all ready when M and Mme knocked at my door. Having paid the landlady the previous night, we slipped out very quietly and made our way to the railway station. It was still dark and there were only a few people about. Of these, some were searching the streets with torches, and I was quite bewildered by their behaviour until I realised that they were collecting cigarette ends. In the station we had a cup of coffee and some more of the sandwiches, which I had brought with me from Sains du Nord.

The train left at 5.00am, and it was a very quiet journey to Arras where we arrived at 7.30am. The only thing particularly interesting en route being a German aerodrome with Focke-Wulf Fw 190s parked on the field. Previously I had seen plenty of German aircraft, but they had all been in the air, and this was my first close-up. Leaving Arras station we separated, I went with M Dumont and Mme went on alone via a different route. By a circuitous route we made our way to a house where we were admitted by Mme, who had arrived earlier. The house was one of a terrace in a very ordinary street, with a sign 'Secours Nationale' above the door. It was the property of Mme but part was rented to this society, which, being a committee organised by Marshal Petain to assist the poor, made it above suspicion and proved to be a very useful blind.

Bale Out!

I was destined to stay in this house for three days before moving on and during which time I learnt something of the history of Mme. She was the wife of an Englishman, who was interned in Germany. They had been married during the First World War and he had subsequently been employed by the Imperial War Graves Commission. It seemed to me that being the wife of an internee she would have been more closely watched by the Gestapo but the risk did not frighten her and she delighted in the fact that she was doing something which would have pleased her husband.

By no means was I the first airman whom she had assisted, as there had been many previously, and I saw photographs of several of them. For Madame Witton, and all the other people who helped me to escape, I still have great admiration. For no amount of money would I have taken their place as continually they were taking risks and always in a state of suspense and uncertainty. How they could stick it I do not know, as I am certain that my nerves would have gone to pieces!

After we had breakfasted on two fried eggs, supplied by Madame's hens, M Dumont left but was to return a few hours later with an American airman, Doug Hoehn.

We certainly were pleased to meet each other, and not a little surprised either. Naturally the first thing we did was to exchange stories. He had been the bombardier in a Flying Fortress attacking an airfield near Arras about a fortnight previously. They had been attacked by a fighter and had been forced to bale out when they were about 25,000 feet up. All the crew had got out of the aircraft, but several had been machine-gunned and killed in the air by the Germans when they were parachuting down. Doug, himself, had refrained from opening his 'chute until he was about 2,000 feet from the ground, and so he fell a long distance from the others and had remained unseen by the Germans. His pilot, incidentally, had also made a delayed jump but unfortunately had waited too long before pulling his rip-cord and had been killed.

For several days Doug had slept in the woods where he landed; then he had contacted some people who had hidden him in a barn, and after staying there for several more days he had been taken to Arras by car. I was very interested in his 'free fall' of over 20,000 feet. Doug had remained fully conscious all the time, in a sort of sitting position with his legs practically level with his head. Apparently by looking over his shoulder he could see the ground coming towards him and so could judge his height. Rather amazingly he said that once, he raised one foot higher than the other to find that it acted as a sort of rudder, so that he turned round and round. Discovering this he amused himself for a short time by first raising one foot and then the other so that he kept turning to the left and then to the right.

This stay in Arras was very pleasant. Doug and I played cards, read books, and listened to the wireless whenever Mme was in the house but, if she was out, we had to keep very quiet so as not to arouse suspicion. M Dumont did not live in the house but visited us once or twice each day, very often with some news about trains having been derailed and other incidents which showed the patriotism of the French people. We also prepared ourselves for the next part of our journey by washing our clothes, pressing our trousers, and making ourselves as respectable as rather odd clothes would allow. In addition we were able to have a warm bath in a large tub, much better than the bucket in which I had previously bathed. One day, too, we had our photographs taken at the open window, and I hoped to be able to collect a copy after the war.

There were just three rooms on the ground floor (which Mme occupied) – one the room where Doug and I slept, then a kitchen, and another room at the back. In order to get to the washroom we had to pass through the kitchen, and one day whilst Doug was at the back there was a ring at the door and Mme brought a man into the kitchen. Doug evidently did not hear the ring or he would have remained quiet where he was, but instead, a few minutes later, he walked into the kitchen in his shirtsleeves and saw Mme talking to a member of the Gestapo in uniform. Doug must have been dumbfounded, but he walked through into the bedroom and closed the door without replying to the man who had said, "Bonjour, Monsieur." That was all there was to the incident (his visit had only been something to do with the rooms which Mme leased), but at

This picture of me (right) was taken at Arras in May 1943 by
Eugene d'Hallendre who was the Chief of Police and also
the Head of the Resistance; he was shot by the Germans in
December 1943. The lady is Mme Rosine Witton and the other
chap is Doug Hoehn, USAF.

the time it worried the three of us quite considerably not knowing whether the man suspected or not.

On two afternoons there were air-raid alarms, very similar to our 'wailing Minnie'. On each occasion it was only fighter intruders and no bombs were dropped, but we were quite disappointed when we did not see any planes.

On Sunday 30 May, the three of us were up very early, getting everything ready for our journey and having a hearty breakfast. At about 8.30am, each complete with tickets, we left the house, Madame Witton first, then Doug, and lastly myself, at minute intervals. Thus in single file, about one hundred yards apart, Madame led us to the station where, because of the crowd, we had to keep closer together. After plenty of jostling we managed to get seats near each other in the train for the three-hour journey to Paris.

The trip was free from all incidents; the only annoying part being the desire of the conductor to check tickets about every half hour. The train was very crowded, with people standing in the central corridors. The man beside me was evidently a black marketeer in cigarettes, as he took down a suitcase filled with them and sold packets to the other passengers in the carriage. Mme bought two packets which she gave to Doug and me later. One thing for which I was very thankful was the fact that all German soldiers travelled in separate carriages.

At 12.30pm we arrived in Paris, at the Gare du Nord and followed Mme off the train through the ticket barrier. Here Mme was met by an elderly lady, to whom we were introduced but whose name I do not remember. The four of us then proceeded down various streets and into a café where we met a gentleman, apparently the head of the organisation, who had been keeping a table for us.

The luncheon which we had was really quite sumptuous, including roast beef, asparagus, potatoes, cherries and the usual red wine, but the number of coupons which the gentleman had to give up was amazing, and so was the amount of the bill, something in the region of 600 francs if I remember correctly. Incidentally I heard that these organisations printed both their own coupons and their own money; certainly there was some hidden source as otherwise such expenditures would have been impossible.

After lunch we had to wait a considerable time until another lady arrived who was going to lead us to a place where we could stay. I spent the time very interestingly by looking out of the window and watching the crowds of people on the streets – Parisians on their weekly holiday with crowds of German soldiers, and a few German girls in uniform, presumably the equivalent of our ATS, or nursing sisters.

One of the things which struck me was the almost complete absence of traffic; I believe that in two hours I only saw two cars, both driven by German officers. The only other vehicles were several horse-drawn cabs, and many tandem and single bicycles pulling little carriages in which were seated two people – these were taxis. Another thing which I found interesting was the fact that many of the people were very well dressed; the war did not seem to have affected their taste or their fashions. Notable was the fact that the very best dressed people were nearly always with Germans.

About 2.30pm we said goodbye to the other people, including Mme Witton, and left the café in company with the lady who had just arrived. She gave us tickets for the Metro, and we followed her down into the station where we caught a train very like those on the London Underground. After travelling for some time we got off, and having walked a short distance we arrived at a block of flats. The lady took us up to the top floor where we were admitted to the apartment. The flat was owned by Mme Le Fevre, a woman of about 25, with a gentleman, John Hannow, a Free French agent, living there temporarily under the same conditions as ourselves. The lady who had brought us from the café was only a friend; she did not live with Mme Le Fevre and had just acted as our guide.

It was a beautiful apartment with lovely furniture, pictures, books and magazines; in addition, as it was at the top of the building, there was an excellent view from the balcony all over Paris. We could see the Eiffel Tower, which was not more than a ½ mile distant and, to remind us of the war, barrage balloons flying on the outskirts of the city sheltering what remained of the Renault works. Staying in this flat was very enjoyable for both Doug and me, as apart from having to stay in our bedroom each day until after the maid had left at 2.00pm, we had absolute freedom and could talk, play the wireless as much as we liked, read English magazines and play cards with Mme and M Hannow. The food, too, was excellent and tasted no worse for having had its origin in the 'black market'.

It was only in Paris that I got some idea of the rationing; in the country things were not so strict but in Paris everything was rationed, even potatoes and salt. Without a large organised 'black market' the people could not have lived. I do not know how the poor people existed, but I did hear cases of rats and cats having been eaten and I do not doubt that these stories were quite true.

If ever I were asked to name the "strangest character I have ever met" I would say M Hannow, or 'John' as I knew him. After France fell he had escaped to England and, being quite young, about 23, had joined the Canadian Navy and served in it for about a year. Then he had been called upon by the Free French Forces, and after receiving special instructions, had been dropped in France by parachute as a secret agent. There John had been head of an organisation specialising in sabotage work. Some of the stories he told Doug and me were stranger than fiction. When we met him he was in hiding from the Gestapo, and was awaiting arrangements to be made for an aeroplane to land in France and take him to England.

His last adventure had been most interesting; he had been arrested by the Gestapo in a house and had been taken for interrogation. They had seated him in the centre of a room whilst a sentry guarded the door, and during the hour he awaited the interrogators he ate all the secret documents which he had had in his pockets when captured. Apparently when his questioners arrived, in the bustle caused by their appearance he had made a dash for the door, grabbed the sentry's rifle, and killed him with the butt. Escaping into the street he ran followed by the pursuers who fired revolvers at him, luckily without injuring him although they killed a woman onlooker. Turning up the first side street he darted into a house and hid himself in an attic. In his hiding place he said that his heart beat so loudly he could hear it, and he had to smash his watch in order to stop its ticking. The Germans searched the house but did not find him, and at night he left the building and escaped completely. Doug and I were curious to know why the Germans had not made a more thorough search of the house. Apparently the Gestapo had not seen him enter, and the people who had did not give him away; one said that he had entered one door and another said another door, consequently the pursuers had to search the entire street.

On the second day of our stay with Mme she took us out into the city to have our identity card photographs taken. The place we went to was a store, something like Woolworth's, and was about a one mile walk from the flat. It was interesting to walk through the streets, although Doug and I felt conspicuous even in our civilian clothes. We had a marvellous view, of the Eiffel Tower, but the thing that amazed me most was the fact that the Parisian women, even under the heel of Germany, seemed to be maintaining their reputation as the best dressed women in the world.

In the store our photographs were taken in an automatic machine, which was anything but private. Mme was with us and she told the girl attendant what we wanted. Unfortunately in positioning me for the 'snap' the attendant wanted me to raise my arm a little; I could not understand what she was saying for some time, but Mme came to my assistance. She apparently told the girl that I had been wounded, the girl evidently thinking that I was a German and I could not speak French.

After the photographs were taken Doug and I walked back to the flat where John let us in. Mme collected the photographic prints in the evening; mine had turned out well, but the camera had become unserviceable when it was Doug's turn and he had to go to another photographer the next day.

On Tuesday we were told that we would be leaving the next day and were given our forged identity cards and other papers. That day, and the next, seemed to pass very slowly, but we spent the time getting everything ready and making ourselves look as respectable as possible.

At last, 6.00pm on 2 June arrived and we left the house, following Mme at intervals of two to three minutes. She led us to the Metro where, as there was a large crowd, we had to stay close together. Boarding a car, we travelled in it for about half an hour and, owing to the fact that it was crowded, I had to stand in the aisle. As luck would have it I was beside a German soldier, who very meekly asked me how to get to a certain place. The only thing I could do was turn my back to him and pretend that I had not heard the question. Luckily he did not repeat it or become offensive; I must have been following the habits of other French people, as although several had heard the question nobody enlightened him.

Finally we got off at an underground station and followed Mme who led us to a group of about four people standing talking. When I was a few yards off I recognised one of them; it was 'Lash', my pilot, and it was all I could do to refrain from rushing up and shaking him by the hand. All we could do was stare at each other with silly grins of pleasure on our faces. The others were all members of the organisation, and two of them were to be our guides on the railway journey. A gentleman led Doug and me out of the station whilst 'Lash' followed with a lady, and after walking a few hundred yards we came to a railway station. The man had the tickets, we passed through the barrier, and onto a train where seats were reserved for us. Then the lady came into our compartment whilst the gentleman evidently travelled with 'Lash' in a different carriage.

At 7.40pm the journey commenced and I felt a great sense of relief as we left Paris, although perhaps it was somewhat ill-founded as there were five strangers in the compartment. Fortunately there was not much talk among the passengers, and neither Doug nor I had any intention of starting a conversation. Doug spent his time with a French book which he did not understand, whilst I had my nose in a magazine, *The Signal*, – in which there was a propaganda article about Éire and how the Irish people were suppressed by the English. I spent a long time translating it and was very interested in finding out how much the attitude of Southern Ireland meant to Goebbels.

Not long after we had started, the lady with us looked across, took out her rail ticket and by signs asked me if I had ours. I shook my head, felt in all my pockets and brought out the seat reservations, but no tickets. Then there started a great panic. I went out into the corridor, she followed and I explained that the man had not given them to me. For some time I thought that Doug and I were as good as captured, but the lady went up the train and after some time came down again, passed me in the corridor and went in and sat down. After she had passed I searched my pockets and discovered two tickets, so dangling them in my fingers I went back into the compartment and took my seat. At once she sat up and started talking to me, much to my consternation, and she showed me two tickets which she had just purchased from the conductor. I had thought that she had slipped the tickets into my pocket as she passed, but they must have been put there by the man who had showed us onto the train. In any case I had been entirely unaware that they were in my pocket. The conversation was of great interest to the other passengers but did not arouse particular attention. After I had made a few monosyllabic replies they all sat back and continued their reading. I felt greatly relieved and no doubt Doug did also, so we relaxed and smoked cigarettes.

Unfortunately another incident was on its way as the lady had kept my ticket but given one to Doug. Perhaps half an hour later Mme left the carriage and two or three minutes later I heard a voice down the carriage demanding tickets. Again I was in a 'flat spin', I kept hoping against hope that the lady would reappear but, no! A man appeared in the doorway saying, "Billets, s'il vous plait."

There was only one thing to do. As he came in I went out not waiting for him to stop me or ask questions. I went up the carriage and started knocking on the door of the ladies room; it was locked but I could not get an answer. After a minute or so the conductor finished collecting in the carriage. He saw me in the corridor and again repeated, "Billet, s'il vous plait, Monsieur." I could not answer but knocked on the door and signed that it was inside. After a moment's hesitation he said, "Ca n'a fait rien!" and passed on. With weak knees I went back to the compartment, sat down and had a cigarette to calm my nerves.

After that we travelled without incident. During the night I dozed, waking at intervals and eating some of the sandwiches I had in a small package. It seemed a never-ending night but at last morning came and about 9.00am we pulled into Limoges. There the train had a stop for about ½ hour, so we got out and had coffee along with the remainder of our sandwiches in the waiting room.

The next major stop for the train was Bordeaux, our destination, where we arrived about 12 noon. There were barrage balloons all round the docks and the bridge across the River Garonne, which we crossed, was guarded by sentries and flak towers.

Doug and I followed Mme out of the station, where we were joined by 'Lash' and his guide. After standing talking for two or three minutes the party was joined by a young man of about 22 who was introduced to us as Francois (Franco); he was to be our new guide. The party then strolled across the street to a little café where we sat at a table on the pavement drinking wine and talking, whilst German soldiers walked past.

After perhaps half an hour we left, walked down a couple of streets and entered a restaurant where we ordered lunch. The six of us sat round a table in the middle of a room, and I know that three of us, at least, were uncomfortable all the time. There were quite a number of people dining, including several Germans and one at least, an officer, kept looking over at us with what seemed more than just casual interest. I felt that the peculiarity of our party must be emphasised by the fact that our three helpers talked quite a lot, whilst the remainder did not open their mouths. However, nothing untoward happened, and about 2.00pm we left and made our way back to the railway station.

Having said goodbye to Mme and M we followed Francois through the barrier and on to another train, which left at 2.30pm for Dax. The journey was quiet but as the train was crowded we had to stand most of the way so I was quite tired when we arrived in Dax about 4.30pm.

Leaving the train we followed Francois, at short intervals, out of the station and, as instructed, I made my way very slowly to a street corner several hundred yards away where the others joined me about five or ten minutes later with four bicycles. Pedalling away, 'Lash' and I followed Doug and Francois at a distance of about two hundred yards and so we cycled for the next few hours. Francois told me later that our exit from Dax had not been so easy as it had seemed. First he had been stopped by a Gestapo man in civilian clothes outside the station and asked for his identity card and then he had had difficulty in getting the four bicycles.

The cycle ride was not to be without incident either – not more than two miles outside the town my chain broke and at the same time 'Lash' got a puncture. We had to stop at the roadside to mend the puncture, and then Francois rode back into the town to change my cycle for another. We hid in the hedge at the side of the road until he returned when we all set off to cover the rest of the way without mechanical trouble at least. It was a long ride, somewhere about 45 miles, made longer by the fact that we had to take a detour as the main route was barricaded off in one village. My bicycle was a very ancient model with quite the hardest saddle I have ever known, and as Francois did not believe in taking it easy it was all I could do to keep up with the pace on that very warm day.

Francois was a very highly-strung individual and seemed to take a dislike to me from the beginning, probably because I was most unlike a Frenchman, especially one from the south and also because my clothes did not look as if they had come from Savile Row. No doubt he was justified, as I must have been far more conspicuous than the others and as such I was an extra risk to him.

Only one little incident occurred when 'Lash', who was behind us all, was stopped by a lorry driver. 'Lash' had not the least idea what the man said but he had replied, "Je ne sais pas" and as it transpired that the man had wanted to know his way this answer was very satisfactory.

We rode on and on, for days it seemed to me, passing through a lovely countryside, no doubt, but little did I appreciate the scenery. At last, about 10.00pm, we came to the outskirts of Bayonne and, after winding our way through side streets, we arrived at an old garage where we hid our bicycles. It was not yet quite dark and we had to walk out into the country for half an hour or so until it was safe for Francois to take us to the place where we were to spend the night. Darkness came and we followed our guide, at intervals, back into the town and into a little riverside café where we were greeted by a very fat man, who was evidently the proprietor. He gave us a tremendous meal – potato omelette, green peas and fried eels with coffee and wine, rather a strange meal but very enjoyable. We all made the most of it, and after cigarettes and a short talk we went to bed feeling very relieved and happy to be once more under a roof and able to enjoy a certain amount of freedom.

Next day, about 12.30pm, we dragged ourselves out of bed, had a meal and then played cards until it was time to continue on our way. Around 6.00pm we made our way out of the café in pairs, 'Lash' and I going to a bridge to await the bicycles which Doug and Francois were going to fetch. After five or ten minutes they arrived and we set off in pairs, 'Lash' and I again riding about 200 yards behind the other two. Leaving the town we rode into the country and had a beautiful view of the Pyrenees against a perfect blue sky. The countryside really was delightful, but that was not to be wondered at as we passed a signpost at a road crossing, which said 'Biarritz 10 Km'.

After riding for perhaps half an hour Francois was joined by another cyclist, a young woman who rode along with him whilst the three of us followed behind. This seemed very strange and risky to me at first, but we found out later that the lady was acting as a blind for Francois in case we should all happen to be stopped.

We rode for about three and a half hours, mainly on small roads and cart tracks, until we arrived at our destination – St Jean de Luz. It was only 9.30pm and not yet dark so we had to waste an hour in and around the town before our last lap over the mountains could commence. 'Lash' and I kept together whilst Doug went along with Francois, the young lady having disappeared. It was very dangerous here, being so close to the border and, to say the least of it, I felt quite excited. We spent most of the time a little way out of the town looking across the bay, watching the fishing boats come in with their day's catch, and also the fishermen on the rocks below us. I think that it is one of the most beautiful places I have ever seen, and it really was especially wonderful under a glorious sunset.

People were passing on the road along side us but nothing happened until a German soldier came and stood at our side. He was watching the fishing too, and after several minutes asked us if the men had caught anything. 'Lash' replied, in what must have been dreadful French, that they had caught a large fish (I had not seen anything longer than about three inches) and indicated the size with his hands. At other times it would have been funny but we were not in a position to appreciate the joke, and after replying we turned away from him, intending to convey that we did not want to speak with him. Anyway nothing more transpired and, after a few minutes of silence, he turned and walked away, much to our relief; I could almost feel my heart slip back to its normal position.

10.30pm came and with it darkness. The four of us made our way down various side streets and out along a railway line, where we met two men who were joining us on the trip across the mountains. They supplied us with sandals, in place of our heavy shoes and cotton trousers, in exchange for those which we had worn. Francois brought our trousers in a pack on his back, but the shoes were to be sent to Paris for the use of boys who might later arrive in a similar way to ourselves with only their flying boots. After a few minutes the five of us set off through fields and along narrow lanes, usually up to our knees in grass, which was damp from the dew. Due to the fact that we avoided all farmhouses we did not seem to go in any particular direction, although after about an hour the mountains were much closer.

About midnight the guides led us to a farmhouse at the foot of the mountains where we rested for half an hour and had some milk and sandwiches. Here, too, we picked up a new guide. He was an amazing man, a Basque, aged about 65 years, with tremendous stamina, as we were to learn. He led us up the mountainside by practically invisible paths for, what seemed to me, hours. We walked at a fast pace through a type of prickly heather which scratched my legs. The weather was very much in our favour; it was a clear starry night without a moon, and quite cold. The cold was a blessing as our climb was, to say the least, somewhat energetic. The mountain was not particularly high and after about two hours we reached the top, from where we could see Spain and the lights of Irun. Then we began to descend, sometimes in woods and sometimes in the heather. There were sheep on the mountain and when we went near them they would scamper away ringing the bells which were tied around their necks.

Finally at 3.20am on Saturday 5 June 1943, we reached the river which was the boundary between France and Spain. Here we had to be especially careful as there might be guards, and we picked our way very cautiously along the river bank until the guide found the place where we could ford the stream. The river was about 30 yards wide at this place, and rather swift flowing, so we all joined hands and started to wade across in a line. The water came up to our thighs, but apart from a few slips on stones it did not give us very much trouble and we all got across safely.

Once over we felt somewhat relieved. 'Lash' and I shook hands but did not speak for fear of guards. On the Spanish side we still had to be careful, because if we had been caught by the police we would have been interned and that would have meant a rather noticeable haircut and two or three weeks in prison until the British authorities could obtain our release.

After leaving the river bank we started to climb once more, first of all crossing a railway, then a road, both of which ran alongside the river. There was very thick undergrowth and whilst walking along the railway I managed to fall down an embankment which had been hidden by the trees and foliage. It was a drop of about ten feet, but apart from creating a lot of noise no harm was done and the others pulled me back to safety.

Now we started to climb our second mountain, but this time it was very different. It was a very steep slope covered by trees and bushes, and the only way we could get up was on our hands and knees. However, after about three-quarters of an hour the slope lessened and the climbing was less difficult. Reaching the top of this second mountain about 5.00am, we paused for a short rest, and then continued the march across a plateau. It was quite easy

TELEPHONE :
GERARD 9234
Extn.................

Any communications on the
subject of this letter should
be addressed to :—

THE SECRETARY,
and the following number
quoted :— P.403044/7/P.4.Cas.B.3.
Your Ref.

AIR MINISTRY

(Casualty Branch)

73-77, OXFORD STREET,

W.1.

16 . June, 1943.

CONFIDENTIAL.

Sir,

    I am directed to inform you that information has been received
from a confidential and reliable source stating that your son Flying
Officer Alfred Martin, Royal Air Force, previously reported missing,
has now arrived in a neutral country.

    This information should be treated as strictly confidential and
should not be released to the press or mentioned on the telephone. In
the interests of your son's safety you are advised not to make further
enquiries or attempt to communicate with him at present. Any further
news received will be immediately communicated to you.

          I am, Sir,
          Your obedient Servant,

          E.J. Clarke

    for Director of Personal Services.

R. Martin, Esq.,
  Sicily Villa,
    Balmoral,
      Belfast,
        Northern Ireland.

At 3.20am on Friday 5 June 1943 our little band reached the French-Spanish border and Spain and, with due care and attention not to attract the interest of the Germans we crossed into Spain. Even then we had to be careful as had we been caught there we would have been interned until the British authorities could obtain our release. Obviously, in the interests of security the Air Ministry could not tell my family where I was, until I was safe on British sovereign territory.

walking now, and having got my second wind I did not feel too exhausted. By this time it was light and we had a wonderful view before us of mountains and valleys fading into the distance on one side and on the other side to the sea about ten miles away.

After walking for about two hours, during which time we passed fortifications and concrete roads begun but never completed in the Civil War, we began to descend the mountain, coming upon farmhouses on the mountainside and in the valley.

About 7.30am we came to one of these farmhouses. Our Basque guide went up to the house, met the farmer and in a few minutes we all went inside where in due course we sat down to breakfast. It was decided that Doug and I would stay at the farm all day, while Francois and 'Lash' went on to San Sebastian where we would join them in the evening. So Doug and I went to bed and tried to sleep. I say tried because both of us were overtired and, in addition, we were forever brushing flies off our noses. Never have I seen so many flies as there were in that house; whilst I was sitting down I am sure that there were never less than twenty on each of my knees.

About five in the evening we got up, had a wash and after having a meal we left with the Basque to meet Francois, who was going to escort us into San Sebastian. We had a two hour walk to Irun – at a rather hectic pace set by the Basque – and there we met Francois, who took us by a street railway into San Sebastian. I have a vivid recollection of that ride because I was violently sick most of the way. My stomach was in an awful condition from irregular meals and all sorts of food and the motion of the tram must have brought on this sickness. All the time I stood leaning over the rail at the end of the car trying to remain inconspicuous from the other passengers, in which object I seemed to succeed.

The ride lasted half-an-hour, then we left the tram and walked (about 25 yards from each other) through the streets of the city until we reached a house not far from the beach. The house belonged to a Spanish man and his wife, and the four of us – Francois, 'Lash', Doug and myself – stayed there for four days until Francois had made arrangements with the British Consul to take us to Madrid.

The whole four days I did not leave the house, although I would have liked very much to explore the city. What I had seen during my walk through it was very beautiful – wide streets with trees along both sides and clean buildings. From one of the windows we could catch a glimpse of the sea and of the beach; it looked very enticing. 'Lash' and Doug went out swimming one afternoon, but I had to stay in as my hair was regaining its redness, which made me noticeably not Spanish. However, it was not an unpleasant stay for we played cards most of the time and had some of the most wonderful food I have ever tasted although my stomach did not let me enjoy it as much as I would have liked.

Finally, on the fourth day, arrangements were completed. We left in the evening, about 10.00pm, following the lady of the house. Doug and I walked some distance behind 'Lash' and the lady along various roads until a car stopped and picked the three of us up. The driver was one of the staff at the British Embassy in Madrid. He was with his wife and together we drove all through the night until we arrived in Madrid next morning. It was an interesting journey because during the night there was a violent thunderstorm, and in lightning flashes we could see the very beautiful countryside just as if there was a short strip of Technicolor in a black and white film. Then in the morning we passed though many villages, over a high mountain range and across a plateau, all the time seeing a people and a countryside so different from anything that I had previously encountered.

About 10.00am we were passing through the streets of Madrid, and shortly afterwards we were having a very welcome breakfast at the house of our friend, the Embassy official. Following breakfast we were taken to the Embassy, where we had an interview. They told us that it would not be possible to get away for a few days, so we asked for, and received, permission to write letters to our parents.

There were several others boys in the Embassy who had had experiences similar to our own – three or four Americans and the remainder RAF – and we spent seven days with them exchanging stories and sunbathing in the garden. It was pleasant and peaceful after our adventures, spoilt only by the desire to know how our

On 23 June 1943 my father received this telegram advising that I had arrived at Gibraltar. I can only imagine what a relief this news must have been to my family.

parents and relatives were keeping. I was disappointed at not being allowed to explore Madrid, but as our presence was unknown to the Spanish authorities that was impossible.

At last the day for departure arrived. We packed all our kit (such as it was) and in the evening we were taken to the train station. The journey to Gibraltar lasted thirty-six hours and was only notable for two things – the terrible dust which accumulated in the carriages and the stops at small country stations where the train was surrounded by women and children selling fruit, water and some type of pastry which seemed to me to be entirely composed of olive oil. Near Gibraltar we got off at a small station and proceeded the remainder of the way in a bus. Passing through the Spanish customs we entered the fortress of Gibraltar and were once more back on home territory.

At Gibraltar we received uniforms and identity cards and became members of a Mess, in which we stayed for four days until they told us that we were being flown back to England. 'Lash' and I were very interested to hear news of both our navigator and wireless operator who had passed through Gibraltar several weeks previously. It was not until we got back to England that we heard with regret that our rear gunner had been killed and that both the engineer and mid-upper gunner were prisoners of war.

The trip to England was uneventful and we landed at Bristol early on the morning of 22 June. Before proceeding to London by train I sent off a telegram to my family and was very pleased to receive a reply as soon as I arrived.

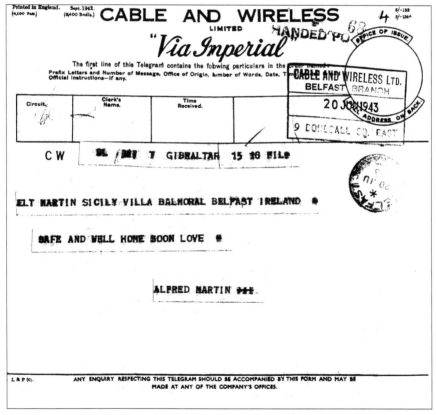

This was probably the telegram that my parents had longed for – from me to say I was safe and on my way back to good old Belfast!

Our stay in London was very short. We had an interrogation and were issued with uniform, travel warrants and leave passes, all in a few hours. It was too late to catch the boat to Ireland that evening but my skipper, 'Lash', and I managed to get to Yorkshire where we visited our Royal Air Force station and received a great welcome from all our friends there. We also gave a big 'thank you' to the WAAFs who had packed our parachutes so well.

Next day I travelled to Ireland. It was wonderful to be home, to see my parents and to spend almost two complete days shaking hands with all the neighbourhood. I got a tremendous welcome but, through it all, I tried to remember with gratitude those people who had made it possible and who were still under the control of the Germans.

Chapter 3:
The outcome, and all is well again
(except for some)

It was 25 June 1943 when I arrived home in Belfast to that wonderful welcome. I guess I was a little like the Prodigal Son, so happy to be back living with my parents, and my sister and my brother. Friends too, crowded in on me, to say hello and shake my hand, some showing surprise and a hesitation about completing their initial remark of "I thought you were, uh . . ."! After a few days things settled down and my extended leave began to follow the normal pattern of get up late, eat, go to parties or dances, stay out late and once again sleep in; just a busy, lazy time, with some special events and visits to make plans for the future.

Early in the leave I made a two day trip to London where I had a medical examination and a discussion about my future. I was told that I would not be allowed to return to operations, in order to avoid any possibility of information being disclosed about the Resistance movement and my helpers in Belgium and France. Frankly, I was not the least unhappy about this operation information, and I promptly applied to be sent on a Staff Navigators course with the view to becoming an instructor. Later in the war evaders, such as I, were permitted, and encouraged, to go on operations but only in different areas of the conflict.

During those first few weeks I had pleasant meetings with the staff in the insurance company where I had worked, The Liverpool and London and Globe Insurance Co Ltd, now an almost forgotten part of the Royal Sun Alliance Group. The company was wonderfully supportive to its members serving in the forces. I received personalised diaries each year containing encouraging messages from the management and, in addition, my pay in the Forces was made up by the company to what it had been when I was called up. That was especially welcome during my time in the Royal Engineers as my basic pay was in the region of 1/3- to 2/0- per day. Later on in the RAF my pay jumped to 7/6- per day plus, and my insurance company salary was left far behind.

Another pleasant get together was with the Council and members of Balmoral Golf Club. They treated me as if I had just won the British Open and was about to have my handicap reduced. I still have a very handsome silver cigarette case engraved with the words "To commemorate a Happy Landing". It awaits recycling should I ever decide to become a smoker again!

Early in July the Headmaster of Friends' School, Lisburn (which I had attended) asked me to present the prizes on Sports Day. I felt honoured but oh so shy. The event is a bit of a blur in my memory, as anything I said was incoherent. Also, I failed to recognise my two cousins, Kathleen and her sister Phyllis, who was one of the prize winners. Hopefully, they have now forgotten my failings.

My father had kept and replied to all the 'obituary' letters expressing hope and sympathy which the family had received. I found them a little embarrassing, but at the same time a tear would come to my eye in thankfulness for all the kind and sincere thoughts. No doubt these letters had given great support to my parents during the time that I was missing.

I will never know exactly but it seemed to me that they had shown remarkable courage and a great determination to find out as much as possible about what had happened. No doubt these efforts gave them strength and, indeed, they learned after many enquiries and help from an aunt and uncle in Yorkshire that Sergeant Laurie Neill, our mid-upper gunner, was a PoW in Germany. Further, a letter to his parents disclosed that I had been first out of the aircraft and therefore I should have survived. This information was passed to my family just a day or two before the first official telegram (see page 73) told of my arrival in Gibraltar. Obviously, for my family, the news must have seemed better and brighter and a wonderful answer to many prayers.

Following the visit to London for the medical examination, I had stopped in Pocklington on my way back home. There I was told that I had been awarded the Distinguished Flying Cross and I also received a congratulatory telegram from Air Chief Marshal Sir Arthur T Harris (reproduced overleaf), all somewhat unexpected, as all I had attempted was to get back home as quickly as possible.

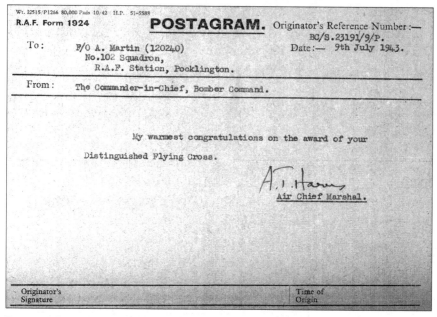

My warmest congratulations on the award of your Distinguished Flying Cross.

A.T.Harris
Air Chief Marshal.

Originator's Signature	Time of Origin

I received a congratulatory telegram from Air Chief Marshal Sir Arthur T Harris during a call at Pocklington en route to Belfast. It was a detail like this that showed why ACM Harris was highly-regarded by his aircrews.

Still, my determination had paid off and I could not help but feel a little pride especially from the pleased reaction from my parents.

At the end of August I was posted to Bishops Court, near Ardglass, Co Down and told to make myself useful until my posting to a Staff Navigator course came through. I was not given any special duties so I filled my time by acting as Assistant Adjutant and Orderly Officer. Socially, it was a very pleasant period. Riding in and out on my bicycle, I enjoyed playing golf at Ardglass and visiting and dining out with a second cousin, Jeanne Addison, who was a school teacher in the village. I was able to reach Belfast by bus via Downpatrick. There I visited my parents and friends whilst making an up to date inventory of all the dance halls around the city and the talent (female) attending thereat.

7 October was a very important day for me, although I did not realise it at the time. That evening I went to a dance at Albert

White's in Belfast. Shortly after my arrival I spotted an attractive 'Wren' across the dance floor and promptly asked her for a dance. Her name was Barbara Murdoch and that dance continues to this day, but it was to be ten years before it became officially recognised. We were married in Canada in December 1953. Both of us tend to agree that it was ten years wasted but I knew I had some more wild oats to sow, and probably Barbara had too. Furthermore my financial position needed much improvement before it would reach the level of "for better" rather than "for worse".

As a Flying Officer my accommodation at Bishops Court was a partitioned area in a Nissen hut. A bed, a chair and a small chest of drawers were the only furnishings. My valuables, such as they were, were kept in the top drawer of the chest. Pilfering did not exist but I discovered that other rascals were around.

Amongst my valuables was the much cherished monthly chocolate ration. Some rascal had been fancying it and in consequence I kept it in the battery area of my bicycle lamp – a safe place, but much scratched by the horde of thieving, hungry, field mice in the neighbourhood; surely a good example of the hardships faced by service men and women during World War II!

At the end of the year my posting came through and on 8 January 1944 I joined many others as a passenger on the French liner *Pasteur* of 29,000 tons displacement. We sailed from Liverpool and after an uneventful journey reached Halifax, Nova Scotia eight days later. From there it was a short train ride to the holding centre at Moncton, where the powers that be took a week to decide that I should move onward to Toronto and thence to the RAF station at Port Albert, near Goderich, on the shores of Lake Huron. It was a lovely station, with a nine hole golf course nearby and excellent mess parties and dances at frequent intervals. It was a time of almost no rationing and no blackouts. The food was first class and well above the standard to which I had become accustomed. Even if Oliver Twist had been in the RAF he could not have asked for more.

This was to be my home for more than a year. Early on I completed my Staff Navigators course with its emphasis on spherical trigonometry and astronavigation, arts that I never really needed to use, as we were moving into the era of radar direction finding with Gee, H2S, etc. However, when I later became an instructor of 'sprog' navigators I did quite a lot of flying training with the pupils and I enjoyed it. Morale amongst the students was very high and their enthusiasm and sense of humour a real joy. On one occasion, flying in an Anson and on the final leg to base, I found one of the pupils peering anxiously over my shoulder into the distance and muttering, "They've moved it the buggers."

Being one of the 'permanent' officers on the station I found myself being more and more involved in the various activities. As well as lecturing on navigation, maps and charts, meteorology and other subjects I was appointed Mess Secretary, which gave me responsibility over the accounts, the catering and general affairs and assets of the mess. The only real Mess problem that I can remember was when the station closed in January 1945. All the equipment was disposed of except for a very fine Berkel Bacon Slicer, the origin of which was unknown and its future unwanted. In the end it was left behind – possibly to originate that old joke about the butcher "who backed into the bacon slicer and got behind in his work".

Amongst the numerous personnel on the station there were two Pilot Officers from Northern Ireland – Philip Horrocks and Charlie Nisbet, the three of us being referred to as 'Paddy'. Philip had worked in the Belfast Harbour Commissioners office prewar whilst 'Chuck' Nisbet had been a teacher and an artist, who had contributed cartoons to *Pro Tanto Quid*, the Queens University students fund raising publication. Additionally he was an excellent 'play by ear' pianist making him very popular at all mess parties where we wanted to sing the dirty ditties of the day, such as *The Ball of Kerrymuir* or *They're shifting Father's grave to build a sewer*.

I was friendly with both of them, but perhaps a little closer to 'Chuck' as he and I went to New York together, where we stayed with his Aunt Belle on Long Island. My memory tells me we were about the most inconsiderate guests of all time – there only between the hours of 2.00am and 10.00am, mostly spent in bed or eating what was made for us, just two 'skivers' who were never invited back. As you will have gathered 'Chuck' was quite a character and friendly towards all, except perhaps if you were having kippers for breakfast; then he would let you be and move to an area of more pleasant smells.

For those of us fortunate enough to be in Canada, 1944 was a very pleasant year. In Europe, on the other hand, D-day and the Normandy landings affected everybody and everything. We could only read about it and do our best to turn out well-trained aircrew to fill the vacancies.

Socially there were very few problems about how to spend our 48 hour passes and several longer periods of leave. Cities such as Toronto, Detroit, Philadelphia and New York could be (and were) visited. I managed to find distant relatives and also to make friends almost everywhere.

In New York I was introduced to the English Speaking Union, an organisation which still exists today. The entertainment and welfare of visiting servicemen was a high priority with it and the hospitality and friendliness was second to none. Forgive me for 'name dropping' if I reminisce about those unforgettable leaves, or furloughs as they should be called – morning dances with the young ladies of Powers Model Agency, lunch with Mrs John D Rockefeller and others, followed by a show at Radio City Music Hall (the film was *National Velvet* starring Elizabeth Taylor), accommodation provided by William S Paley, head of CBS, in his apartment in downtown Manhattan, cocktails with Betty Whitney, a visit to the Latin Quarter nightclub and an afternoon on the roundabouts at Coney Island – all quite fabulous for someone who had previously thought that a Saturday night at the Carlton Dance Hall in Belfast was the zenith of high living.

There was another side to this wonderful hospitality. One of the lady helpers talked to me for a short time and then said she would (and did) write home to my mother to tell her about our meeting and how I looked, etc, – surrogate mothering, which I know pleased my mother.

Bale Out!

Probably I benefited greatly from all the travel and the exposure to a different way of life. Certainly I learned something during a trip to Cleveland. I was on my own; I did not have friends there, and I only went because it was an important city which I had not visited before. One sunny morning sitting on a bench in a park I waited for something to happen. It did; a gentleman of about 40 joined me on the bench and we chatted for some time exchanging information about ourselves. I gathered that he ran a small cosmetic manufacturing business and that he was a bachelor, whilst I told him of my love for golf and the hope that I could get a game in Cleveland. He suggested we should visit his house and then he would see what could be done about playing golf. He lived in a very fine, modern, house, but I quickly learned that he was much more interested in showing me his bedroom than taking me out for golf. Yes, I was very naïve, but the penny did eventually drop and I beat a hasty retreat with as much dignity as possible. Back at my hotel I got over my fright and vowed never again to be taken in so easily.

In February, I was posted to Malton, outside Toronto, to what is now Lester B Pearson International Airport! Why I was sent is a mystery, as I had no duties except to eat, drink, sleep, and visit my friends in the area. It also gave me a chance to catch up on my correspondence, which was considerable. Some young ladies whom I had met in the past got letters, as well as my parents who were written to every Monday evening without fail. The only exceptions I remember were during the period I was on the run in Europe. On 22 November 1944 having heard that the Allied Armies had overrun the Ardennes, I had written to the Coolens in Sains du Nord to tell them of my safety. No reply had been received by the time of my arrival in Malton, so I sent off further letters to André Leleu in Sivry, Belgium and to Mme Lagersie in Lille.

On 1 April 1945 I travelled overnight by train from Toronto to Winnipeg and on to my new posting at Portage la Prairie, a very pleasant prairie town, near enough for me to play golf in Winnipeg and stay with friends at their summer retreat in Gimli on Lake Winnipeg. It was very pleasant swimming despite the presence of numerous mosquitoes and black flies which enjoyed the pastures of my pale young skin. The war in Europe and my war were slowly coming to an end. I lectured to various courses and also acted as Welfare Officer on the station. There was very little flying and plenty of time off.

In July a friend and I invested $25.00 each in railroad tickets and set off on a ten day leave. The tickets were a special issue for service personnel and entitled us to travel anywhere in Canada and return. Our choice was Vancouver but we never made it that far. Getting off the train at Banff we spent two days at Lake Louise enjoying the great beauty of the Lake, the glacier and the mountains. The tranquility of the area was wonderful but for two boys on leave a little more was required. We returned to Banff to spend the rest of our leave playing golf in the luxurious surroundings and enjoying the company of other service people, mainly Royal Canadian Air Force, in the evenings. The Banff Springs Hotel was closed but the King Edward was more than adequate for our needs. A convertible Cadillac taxi took us to the golf course in the mornings; the course was superb with lots of wildlife to be seen, and avoided. Elk and moose grazed the fairways and kindly refrained from running off with our balls.

Shortly after returning to Portage La Prairie, a General Election was held in the United Kingdom and I was appointed Electoral Officer, to look after the voting entitlement of the 100 or so UK subjects on the station. After almost six years away from home I had little knowledge or interest in political affairs and even as Electoral Officer the whole procedure was a bit of a non-event for me. It was with amazement that I learned that the Labour Party had been returned, that our superb leader, Winston Churchill, had been defeated and that someone called Attlee was now Prime Minister.

A few days later we celebrated VJ Day with a general celebration and party in the camp. That to us was also a bit of a non-event, but it heralded the beginning of demilitarisation, and for many the word 'demob' began to appear on the distant horizon.

It was 28 August 1945 when I learned that I was posted to Moncton, New Brunswick en route to discharge. In a languid sort of way things began to move quite quickly. First I went to Winnipeg for a few days, where I shopped for nylons and other scarce items which might be used for gifts or bribes. Then it was Toronto for two weeks. My faulty memory now recalls that it was at this time that I took that almost 'sexy' visit to Cleveland as described on page 85. After Toronto there followed two nights in Montreal, where I paid a visit to the Canadian Head Office of the insurance company I had worked for prewar. (All options for the future had to be kept open). My arrival in Moncton was on 20 September and my stay lasted until 4 October, when a group of us took the train to Halifax, boarded the French transatlantic liner *Ile de France* and set sail for Europe about 10.30pm that evening.

The crossing took six days, uneventful and comfortable. On the morning of 10 October we called at Cherbourg and then docked at Southampton some hours later. That evening we were passed through Customs and on to a train at 11.00pm. Next day we arrived at Harrogate where I was billeted at Ashfield College, very glad of the rest from travelling and delighted to be able to visit my aunts, uncles and former friends in this lovely Yorkshire oasis, or should I say spa.

Two months of dithering followed. First I was sent to West Kirby for two hours (!) before I was off on leave to Belfast via Carlisle and Stranraer. There I got my 1932 Riley car started and on the road, ready to take out that nice Wren, Barbara Murdoch, whom I had met almost exactly two years earlier. Then, it was back to Catterick just to report, Belfast again for ten days before another Catterick visit and a medical for discharge purposes. There were to be two more visits to Catterick and a final few hours at Hednesford, near Birmingham, before my final release. It was 6.30pm on 18 December 1945 when I was demobbed, complete with grey pinstripe suit, discharge papers and a very modest amount of pound notes in my pocket. No doubt history will decide whether my time in the Services was value for money to the war effort or whether it was money wasted on frivolous living. All I know is that I enjoyed it; it was an experience, I did my best and, damn it, 60+ years on I would be proud of the opportunity to do it all again.

The time has now come to think of the many people who helped me to evade capture, to remember their hospitality and their courage and in a number of cases to record their sacrifices.

First and foremost are the Coolens of Sains du Nord, not far from the French-Belgian border and about 15 kilometres from Epsauvage where we were shot down. I had written to M Coolen on 22 November 1944 but did not receive a reply until he wrote on 7 May 1945. Here is a translation of that letter:

Dear Alfred

We have just received with great joy the good news that you are in good health. After such a long silence we were beginning to fear the worst, but now we are reassured. Your letter dated November 20th took almost six months to reach us. I hope that this one will get to you quicker. Here we are all in good health. Maria is married and living in Belgium. René has been soldiering since the invasion of Normandy. He was in the Belgian Ardennes at the time of the German counterattack in December 1944, and we have no news of him since. You will remember Monsieur de Lille take you away from our house with the woman who spoke English; a short time after, he was arrested by the Germans and shot. His wife was put in a German camp and his son sent to prison in Brussels, from which he has been liberated by the English. Long life and happiness to Madame Fernand and Mlle Adele who will be very happy to receive you if one day you come to France. We have just heard this moment by the CSJ that the war in Europe is ended. I have also just received your letter sent on by Mlle Lagersie de Lille, who is also delighted to know you are alive.

Thanks for having thought of sending us your news.

Hoping to see you again one day and renew our best friendships.

Best wishes to your parents, your brother and sister

Eugene Coolen

It was a great experience for me to visit them after the war, first in 1953, with my sister Dorothy, travelling to Sains du Nord via Brussels. Later, in 1976, I drove to Paris with my wife, Barbara, for an Escaping Society reunion. We travelled via Larne–Stranraer and Dover–Calais to Sains du Nord. The Coolens gave us a great welcome and M Coolen was very pleased to show me the place of our crash at Epsauvage.

M and Mme Coolen are both now deceased, but the family remain, with Jeanne and Leon living in the farmhouse where I was sheltered. I have managed to keep in touch with them at Christmas and on special occasions ever since 1945. In 2003 I was able to send some flowers to Jeanne to commemorate the 60th anniversary of my arrival at Sains du Nord, a small token to acknowledge the great courage shown by them and by all the members of the Resistance in France, Belgium and elsewhere.

André Leleu was the 12-year-old Belgian boy who gave me that very heart warming salute upon discovering me in hiding whilst chasing a cow. The gesture did a very great deal to raise my spirits, which had been very depressed after being shot down about six hours earlier. I visited him in 1976 having corresponded with him before that. He had survived the war without too many problems and appeared to be prospering in the clothing trade. I was able to regain possession of my flying boot, which in 1943 had been left with him as part exchange for a civilian jacket. The boot had provided a comfortable bed for André's dog over all those years. Said boot is now on exhibit at Eden Camp, Malton, North Yorkshire. Recently, a letter which I sent to him was returned marked not known but further enquires have discovered him to be fit and well and living at a different address. Both of us are pleased to be in touch once more.

M Coolen's letter mentions "Monsieur de Lille take you away from our house . . ." That was M Dumont who, along with Mme Witton, escorted me away from Sains du Nord to Lille and then to Arras. As recorded, some months later he was arrested and shot and his wife and son were imprisoned. Probably someone they knew gave them away. Mme Le Fevre, who sheltered Douglas

Hoehn and me in Paris, was a lady of about 30 years who had run a 'safe house' for people on the run (like us), and also as a base for saboteurs and other operators working with the Resistance. A week or so after we left she was picked up by the Gestapo and interrogated daily for six months about giving aid to the enemy. However she never would admit anything and finally they released her. She was convinced that it was her landlady who had 'shopped' her to the Germans.

After our return to Britain I lost track with Douglas Hoehn and it was only years later, in the mid-sixties, when I was living in Canada, that I had reason to try to contact him. Madame Rosine Witton was to visit Canada as a guest of the RAF Escaping Society (Canadian Branch) and wanted to meet anyone whom she had helped. All I could remember about Doug was that he had been in the US Eighth Air Force and had worked in a garage/service station in Eau Claire, Wisconsin. I wrote in January 1967 to the Chief of Police at Eau Claire, asking about Doug's whereabouts. Ten days later I had a reply stating that he was presently living at an address in Chicago. We had a very happy and nostalgic reunion with Mme Witton the following September. A letter which I received from Douglas in 1967 gave me some information which he had obtained during a visit he had made to France after the war. I cannot do better than to quote from the letter:

> You will remember 'John' of the saboteur division. I saw him and had dinner with him after he contacted me, when I got back. I think you should know that he was killed during the invasion of southern France. He parachuted out of a light plane on a mission to close a pincer on the Hun, and was mistakenly shot down by his own troops.
>
> Mme Le Fevre told me that the lady that helped us out of Paris (and on the train to Bordeaux) was shot when she assisted on a similar mission. She never should have been in that business. She was too nervous! But who wasn't?

Remembering the flap on the train about my missing ticket, I cannot help but agree with Doug's comments, although the courage and patriotism she showed were outstanding and never to be forgotten.

'Franco', whose real name was Jean Notholm, was a student during those war years. He survived to take Holy Orders as a priest, first in Detroit and, more recently, in Rome. His many trips as a guide across the Pyrenees and the Spanish border brought safety to many airmen and other refugees. He was honoured by the award of the DSO and is still honoured today as a special guest at various reunions.

The Basque, 'Florentino', who was the guide for those nightly hikes over the Pyrenees and the wades across the Bidasso river, also survived the war. A most impressive figure, he towered over the rest of us and pushed on regardless. It was his determination that led to so many successful border crossings. His award of a DSO was most deserved.

There were other helpers who were in the background and whom I did not meet. To them, too, I say "Thanks!"

Lastly, there was Madame Rosine Witton, the lady who guided me from the Coolen's farm at Sains du Nord to Arras, where she sheltered Doug and me for five days before taking us on to

The Basque, Florentino Goïcoechea (right) and his sons. Florentino guided 227 airmen safely over the Pyrenees and into Spain

Paris. Her husband, an Englishman, was employed in France by the Commonwealth War Graves Commission. At the start of the Second World War he was interned in Germany and remained there until released by the Allies in 1945.

It is probable that Rosine felt lonely during his absence and, as a consequence, she drifted into small acts of resistance such as distributing tracts. Eventually these led to her being 'employed' by the Comete Line to run a 'safe house' and to act as a guide, a very dangerous occupation and one requiring abundant courage. The Comete Line operated from its base in Brussels through Paris to Bayonne and over the Spanish border to San Sebastian. Many hundreds of airmen and other refugees owed their freedom to this wonderful organisation, and of these, Rosine looked after about 70.

Madame Witton operated until December 1943 when, having had to move to Paris, she felt a hand on her shoulder and heard a German voice telling her she was under arrest. She said little about her interrogation but no doubt it was strict as it led to her being sent to Ravensbrück concentration camp. There she remained until 20 May 1945 when she was liberated by the Americans. She never said much about her treatment in Ravensbrück, but from what she did disclose, it was obvious that survival depended on one's relationship with the guards.

She returned, on her own, to Arras, as her husband had been repatriated to London. He was very ill and confined to hospital; she was able to visit him for a few days before his death. This was the terrible outcome of five years' internment. Madame Witton never remarried but lived on a war pension, supplemented by working as a stewardess on cross-channel ferries. I made contact with her in 1967 when I was living in Canada. Along with eleven other helpers from seven European countries she was invited to Canada by the RAF Escaping Society (Canadian Branch) as part of its Centennial Project. She stayed with us at Port Credit, outside Toronto, when all the family enjoyed her company and her recollections of 25 years earlier.

There were to be other meetings with her during visits to France and reunions of the Escaping Society. Usually these were held in the British Embassy in Paris where we all enjoyed the nostalgic chatter, fuelled by the very best champagne. The company was always very interesting and included on one occasion Peter Townsend, who conversed with us about the 'Troubles' and his many visits to Northern Ireland.

Madame Witton died in 1995 at the age of 89, without family but with many friends in the Resistance. She donated her medals, which included the George Medal, to the Imperial War Museum in London. On 13 September 1996 I had the great honour, in company with many members of the French Resistance movement, to present the medals to the Museum. Rosine was a remarkably courageous lady who will never be forgotten by me and by many other people who had the great fortune to call her a helper and a friend.

These were the most prominent of my helpers, but there were many others, including my parents, my sister and brother, relatives in England and some whose names were never known to me. But perhaps above all I should thank the Almighty for providing me with that vital opportunity to evade capture.

Having reached the age of 85, and with the support of my loving wife Barbara, my two daughters Julie and Sheila, and grandsons Max and Grant, I still find it hard to believe how fortunate I have been in my choice of friends and especially my helpers.

To all a sincere thanks and God Bless.

Alfie Martin
Belfast
September 2005

On Tuesday 13 September 1996, British and French friends of Mme Rosine Witton gathered at the Imperial War Museum, London to remember her.

I was privileged to present Rosine Witton's medals and a necklace I had given, along with a copy of the photograph on page 58, to the Imperial War Museum at that gathering.

Our guide from Bordeaux towards the border with Spain was a highly-strung individual called Francois (Franco). He is seen here at Brussels in 2001 with Wally Lashbrook, who had been the pilot of HR 663.

In 1995, fifty years after the end of the war, I was able to attend celebrations in Paris where I met up with my old pilot, Wally Lashbrook. Thankfully, ten years later, I'm still going strong and hope to go back to France to visit the crash site.

The Helpers (as they were in 1967!)

(taken from the Official Programme produced by the RAFES (Canadian Branch) for the Centennial Visit of Helpers)

Madame Anne Brusselmans, M.B.E. (Belgium) was born at Liège and is now living at Brabant. She was involved in all kinds of resistance work, including a connection with M19, British Intelligence and with Belgian Security. The "Comete" line, of which she was a member, returned 800 Airmen and Soldiers to the allied forces. Personally, she sheltered and aided 176 Canadians, Americans, Poles and Britons. This work was carried out between 1941 and 1944, whilst at the same time Mme. Brusselmans was working for the underground press "Libre Belgique" and passing information to "Marc", a Military Information Service. She is the holder of high decorations from Belgium, the United Kingdom, the United States and Poland. Mme Brusselmans is the Society's representative in Belgium.

Signora Maria Carbona (Italy) is now a housewife living in Naples. She has raised two sons, one a lawyer, the other a chemical engineer. During the war, she worked independently with other townspeople, giving shelter, food and clothes to escaping Canadians, Britons and Americans. Her work remained secret, even though she was interrogated. She remarks "My greatest reward was to learn that men safely reached their homes".

Mlle Mabel Fraipont (Belgium) is of Belgian and English parentage. She first made the acquaintance of Canadians when soldiers were billeted at her house during World War I. In World War II, she became a member of an organization in the Province of Liège to assist shot-down allied airmen to escape. As a guest at dinners for high-ranking German Officers, she obtained valuable information. Her father and mother were arrested and condemned. She continued to work against the Germans, visiting prisons to obtain information and assisting allied airmen to escape. Currently in semi-retirement.

Johannes Bernordus ter Haar, B.E.M. (Holland) was born in 1917 at Lichtenvoorde, Holland. An electrician by trade, he worked in the Dutch underground from 1940 to 1944. He assisted 70 Canadian and Allied airmen to escape from Holland, and approximately 350 Belgian and French prisoners of war. His decorations include the British Empire Medal, the Medal of Freedom and the Croix de Guerre. Currently he is an officer in the State Police.

Kjell Harmens (Norway) was born in Lillehammer, Norway, in 1922. He served in the Norwegian underground from May, 1944, until the end of the war. Acted as liaison man and interpreter for a group at Os, which sheltered the Canadian crew of a crashed Wellington bomber and returned them safely to Britain. He stresses that he is only a representative of the many Norwegian helpers.

Mr. Harmens is now employed at Bergen as a manager of purchasing.

François Kerambrun (France) was too old and had too large a family to be mobilized in World War II. His only chance to aid France was to work in the French Underground. He was involved in several organizations in Brittany, including the Shelburn Reseau (Operation Bonaparte) when he transported many allied airmen in his truck, as part of the escape. That operation returned 135 allied airmen to Britain by Motor Torpedo Boats. Decorations include the Croix de Guerre and the Medal of Freedom. He now operates a Service Station.

Henri M. F. Maezelle (France) was born in Gironde in 1919. As a junior officer in the French Army, he was taken prisoner in June, 1940. In April, 1944, he and an Englishman escaped from a German prison camp. Upon returning to France, he operated in the underground and with his family helped allied airmen to evade capture. He guided these evaders from Lille through Paris to Lyon. Now married, he is a Champagne and Wine Merchant in Paris.

Pierre Lucien Noyon (France) was born in 1920, at Calais.

Whilst working on his father's farm in 1943, he encountered a downed Canadian bomber pilot, sheltered him for ten days and provided him with civilian clothing, false papers and money so that he could make his way to the Spanish border.

Mr. Noyon was later deported to a discipline camp in Austria. He is now a manufacturer.

Mlle Claire Peters (Luxembourg) was thrown out of school by the Nazis in 1941 and had to work in a factory for 2½ years. She conveyed escaping airmen to Brussels and supplied them with Belgian identity cards. Was betrayed whilst doing this work and had to flee to Belgium in 1943 and to Switzerland in 1944. After the war she studied law in Paris, worked as a Barrister and Public Prosecutor, and in 1966 was appointed a Judge at Luxembourg.

Aksel Petersen (Denmark) was born in Copenhagen in 1897. Now a Retired Police Inspector. He joined the "Speditorerne" escape group in 1943, contacting and accommodating escaping airmen at Helsingor, passed them to Copenhagen and thence to Sweden. He was assisted in this work by two sons. One of the sons was sentenced to death and shot in April, 1945. Aksel and the other son had to flee to Sweden. He says "Have refused medals, I have only done what I had to do".

Willem Poorterman (Holland) was born at Weirden 44 years ago. He was a very young man at the outbreak of war, and went into hiding to avoid forced labour in Germany. As a member of the Dutch Inland Military forces, he was active in resistance work; helping many airmen to escape, in addition to Jews and forced labour escapees. He specialized in forging signatures for documents. His father was arrested, but later freed. He helped issue resistance newspaper "Trouw" (Faithful), which continued as a daily newspaper after the war. Still employed there as a sports reporter.

Countess Geneviève De Poulpiquet (France) gave shelter to a number of evading airmen, Canadian, British and American. She worked with the Pat O'Leary escape line and was connected with the "Shelburn/Operation Bonaparte" escapes. Visited by the Gestapo in March 1943, her husband was arrested, condemned to death, and died in a German prison in August, 1943. Now living in Paris where she has been doing welfare work, she possesses decorations from France, the United Kingdom and the United States.

Miss Alexandra Poumpoura, M.B.E. (Greece) was a law student when war broke out in Greece. She joined the Greek Red Cross as a volunteer nurse in 1940 and later served at hospitals housing British prisoners of war. She assisted prisoners to escape from hospital, provided shelter and means of escape from the country. In all, she helped 100 Allied servicemen to escape. She and her brother were imprisoned and ill-treated by the enemy. She was awarded the M.B.E. by King George VI. Still with the Greek Red Cross, she was recently on a mission to Jordan.

Miss Poumpoura is the Society's representative in Greece.

Mme Rosine Witton, B.E.M. (France) of Wimereux, Pas De Calais; was born near Arras. She started helping Allied troops left behind from Dunkirk and was connected with the O'Leary and Comete escape lines. She conveyed airmen from Arras to Paris, and when warned of impending arrest, continued to help between Paris and Bordeaux. Arrested January, 1944, she was sent to Ravensbruck Concentration Camp and liberated in May, 1945. She was married to a British subject who was deported to Germany in 1940. He returned to England in 1945 in poor health. Mme Witton joined him in London before his death in August, 1945. She now lives alone on a pension.

April Sky Design is part of the Colourpoint Group.